ROYAL COURT

Royal Court Theatre presents

THE SWEETEST SWING IN BASEBALL

by Rebecca Gilman

First performance at the Royal Court Jerwood Theatre Downstairs
Sloane Square, London on 25 March 2004.

D1353951

THE SWEETEST SWING
IN BASEBALL

by **Rebecca Gilman**

Cast in order of appearance
Roy/Gary **John Sharian**
Dana **Gillian Anderson**
Erica/Dr. Stanton **Kate Harper**
Brian/Michael **Demetri Goritsas**
Rhonda/Dr. Gilbert **Nancy Crane**

Director **Ian Rickson**
Designer **Hildegard Bechtler**
Lighting Designer **Howard Harrison**
Sound Designer **Ian Dickinson**
Composer **Peter Salem**
Assistant Director **Maria Aberg**
Assistant Designer **Luke Wilson**
Casting Director **Lisa Makin**
Production Manager **Paul Handley**
Stage Manager **Tariq Rifaat**
Deputy Stage Manager **Leila Jones**
Assistant Stage Manager **Hannah Ashwell Dickinson**
Stage Management Work Placement **Katherine West**
Costume Supervisor **Iona Kenrick**
Dialect Coach **Joan Washington**
Company Voice Work **Patsy Rodenburg**

The Royal Court would like to thank the following for their help with this production:
Michael Craig Martin, Antoni Malinowski, Donald Morris-Vincent at BaseballSoftballUK, Dr Cleo Van Velsen.

THE COMPANY

Rebecca Gilman (writer)
For the Royal Court: Boy Gets Girl, Spinning into
Butter, The Glory of Living.
Other theatre includes: Spinning into Butter
(Goodman Theatre/Lincoln Center Theater/Seattle
Rep/Alliance Theatre/St. Louis Rep); Boy Gets Girl
(Goodman Theatre/Manhattan Theatre Club); Blue
Surge (Goodman Theatre/The Public Theater).
Awards include: Roger L. Stephens Award from the
Kennedy Center Fund for New American Play
(Spinning into Butter); Finalist for Pulitzer 2002;
Guggenheim Fellowship 2001, the 1999 Evening
Standard Award for Most Promising Playwright, &
joint winner of the 1999 George Devine Award.

Maria Aberg (assistant director)
As assistant director for the Royal Court: The Sugar
Syndrome.
Other theatre includes: Shakespeare Love Songs
(Globe Theater, Neuss, Germany); Romeo & Juliet
(Malmo Dramatiska Teater, Sweden); Laughing Wild
(Friends of Italian Opera, Berlin); In the
Summerhouse (Intima Teatern, Malmo Sweden).
As a director, theatre includes: Duff Luck (Arcola);
My Best Friend (Central Station); A Handful of Dust
(Institute of Choreography & Dance, Cork); The
Maids (Judi Dench Theatre); The Lover (Mountview
Studio).
Maria is a senior script reader for the Royal Court.

Gillian Anderson
Theatre includes: What the Night is For (Comedy);
The Philanthropist (Long Wharf Theatre, New
Haven, Connecticut); Absent Friends (Manhattan
Theatre Club); A Flea in Her Ear (The Blackstone
Theatre); Serious Money, Last Summer at Bluefish
Cove, Romeo & Juliet, In a Northern Landscape
(The Goodman Theatre School); And a Nightingale
Sang (Actor's Theatre).
Television includes: X-Files.
Film includes: House of Mirth, Dancing About
Architecture, The X-Files Movie, The Mighty,
Chicago Cab, The Turning.
Awards include: 1990-1991 Theater World Award
(Absent Friends), 1997 Emmy Award, 1996 Golden
Globe Award, 1996 & 1995 SAG Awards for Best
Actress in a Dramatic Series (X-Files), 2000 BAFTA
Independent Award for House of Mirth.

Hildegard Bechtler (designer)
For the Royal Court: Blood, Terrorism,
Blasted, The Changing Room.
Other theatre includes: The Goat or Who is
Sylvia? (Almeida);The Master Builder (Albery);
The Merchant of Venice, Richard II, King Lear
(RNT); La Maison de la Puppé (Theatre de
l'Europe, Paris); Footfalls (Garrick); The St.
Pancras Project (LIFT); Electra (RSC/Riverside
/Bobigny, Paris); Hedda Gabler (Abbey,
Dublin/ Playhouse, London); Coriolanus
(Salzburg Festival).
Opera includes: The Ring Cycle: Das
Rheingold, Walküre, Siegfried &
Götterdämmerung (Scottish Opera/Edinburgh
Festival); Lady Macbeth of Mtsensk (Sydney
Opera House); Paul Bunyan (ROH); War &
Peace, Boris Gudonov, Peter Grimes,
Lohengrin, The Bacchae (ENO); Dialogues
Des Carmelites (Japan/Paris Opera); Simon
Boccanegra, Peter Grimes (Staatsoper,
Munich); Don Carlos, Wozzeck, Katya
Kabanova (Opera North); Don Giovanni
(Glyndebourne); La Wally (Bregenz
Festival/Amsterdam Musik Theatre).
Film and television includes: The Merchant of
Venice, Richard II, The Wasteland, Hedda
Gabler, Coming Up Roses, Business As Usual.

Nancy Crane
For the Royal Court: Our Late Night, The
Strip.
Theatre includes: Habitat (Royal Exchange);
The Wedding Story (Soho/national tour); Six
Degrees of Separation (Sheffield Crucible);
Absolution (BAC); Angels in America,
Perestroika (RNT); Walk on Lake Erie
(Finborough Theatre); Threesome (Gay
Sweatshop); Oh Hell! (Lyric Studio); Last of
the Red Hot Lovers (Derby Playhouse);
Caligula (Boulevard Theatre); Never The
Sinner (Belgrade Theatre).
Television includes: Cambridge Spies, Strike
Force, Last Days of Patton, 92 Grosvenor
Street.
Film includes: The Machinist, The World of
Tomorrow, The Fourth Protocol.
Radio includes: The Ideal Heroine, Ice Blonde,
The Weight of Water, The Country, The Strip.

Ian Dickinson (sound designer)
For the Royal Court: Notes on Falling Leaves, Loyal Women, The Sugar Syndrome, Blood, Playing the Victim, Fallout, Flesh Wound, Hitchcock Blonde (& Lyric), Black Milk, Crazyblackmuthafuckin'self, Caryl Churchill Shorts, Imprint, Mother Teresa is Dead, Push Up, Workers Writes, Fucking Games, Herons, Cutting Through the Carnival.
Other theatre includes: Port (Royal Exchange, Manchester); Night of the Soul (RSC Barbican); Eyes of the Kappa (Gate); Crime and Punishment in Dalston (Arcola Theatre); Search and Destroy (New End, Hampstead); Phaedra, Three Sisters, The Shaughraun, Writer's Cramp (Royal Lyceum, Edinburgh); The Whore's Dream (RSC Fringe, Edinburgh); As You Like It, An Experienced Woman Gives Advice, Present Laughter, The Philadelphia Story, Wolks World, Poor Superman, Martin Yesterday, Fast Food, Coyote Ugly, Prizenight (Royal Exchange, Manchester).
Ian is Head of Sound at the Royal Court.

Demetri Goritsas
For the Royal Court: Boy Gets Girl.
Other theatre includes: His Girl Friday, A Prayer for Owen Meaney, Finding the Sun (RNT); Rumours of Our Death (Epicentre Theatre); Amadeus (Theatre North West); Noises Off (First Impressions); Twelfth Night (Vogue Theatre); Assassins (Manchester Library); Street Scene, Simon Boccanegra (ENO).
Television includes: Search, The Real Bob Steel, Baddiel's Syndrome, Breaking News, The New Addams Family, Viper, Millennium, The Sentinel, Smudge, The Angel of Pennsylvania Ave, Double Play, A Dream is a Wish, Two, Highlander, Hawkeye.
Film includes: Thunderbirds, Sky Captain & the World of Tomorrow, Deadwood, Spy Game, The Bourne Identity, Duck Ugly, Saving Private Ryan, House Arrest, Excess Baggage, Little Women.

Kate Harper
For the Royal Court: 2 Samuel 11, Under the Clock, Lower Depths, Happy Birthday Wanda Jane.
Other theatre includes: The Trestle at Pope Lick Creek (Southwark Playhouse); The Split (Edinburgh Festival); Cahoots (Mill at Sonning); Fatal Attraction (West End); Liz & Dylan (tour).
Television includes: Wavelengths, Space Precinct, Frank Stubbs Presents, Inspector Morse, Capital City, Poirot, The Upper Hand, Perfect Scoundrels, Pulaski, Hedgehog Wedding, The Two Mrs Grenvilles, Bergerac, Tender is the Night, Oppenheimer.
Film includes: Stiff Upper Lips, Surviving Picasso, Passion of Darkly Noon, Night Watch, Dinosaurs, Batman, Murder Story, Invitation to the Wedding, Reds, Little Lord Fauntleroy.
Kate is a founder member of the Magic Theatre of San Francisco.

Howard Harrison (lighting designer)
Theatre includes: Mamma Mia! (West End, Broadway, Las Vegas, Hamburg, Holland, Japan, Toronto, Australia & US tour); Skellig (Young Vic); Suddenly Last Summer (Sheffield and tour); Matthew Bourne's The Nutcracker (Sadlers Wells & tour); Cat on a Hot Tin Roof (Broadway); Ragtime (Piccadilly); The Master Builder (Albery); The Witches of Eastwick (Theatre Royal, Drury Lane/Prince of Wales); Cat on a Hot Tin Roof (Lyric); A Delicate Balance (Theatre Royal); Black Comedy (Comedy); Putting It Together (Broadway), Henry VIII, Cyrano de Bergerac, The Merchant of Venice, The Tempest, Timon of Athens (RSC); Private Lives, Look Back In Anger, Sleep With Me (RNT); Tales From Hollywood, Privates on Parade, The Vortex (Donmar).
Opera and dance includes: Il Trovatore, Aida, I Masnadieri, Otello (ROH); Beatrice & Benedict, Cavalleria Rusticana/Pagliacci (Welsh National Opera/Opera Australia); Swan Lake, Romeo & Juliet (English National Ballet); Albert Herring (Opera North); The Elixir of Love (ENO); The Makropulos Case, Nabucco (Metropolitan Opera, NY).
Awards include: 2001 Australian Green Room Award (Mamma Mia!), nominated four times Laurence Olivier Awards, Best Lighting Designer.

Ian Rickson (director)

For the Royal Court: Fallout, The Night Heron, Boy Gets Girl, Mouth to Mouth (& Albery), Dublin Carol, The Weir (Jerwwod Theatre Upstairs, Jerwwod Theatre Downstairs & Broadway), The Lights, Pale Horse and Mojo (& Steppenwolf Theatre, Chicago) Ashes & Sand, Some Voices, Killers (1992 Young Writers Festival), Wildfire.

Other theatre includes: The Day I Stood Still (RNT); The House of Yes (The Gate, London); Me and My Friend (Chichester Festival Theatre); Queer Fish (BAC); First Stroke (Soho Poly).

Opera includes: La Serva Padrona (Broomhill). Ian Rickson is Artistic Director at the Royal Court.

Peter Salem (composer)

For the Royal Court: Ashes and Sand. Theatre includes: Passage to India, The Clearing (Shared Experience); Unscrew (The Hopscotch Theatre Co.); War & Peace, A Midsummer Night's Dream, The Miser, The Crucible (RNT); Murder in the Cathedral, Julius Caesar, Victoria (RSC); Mill on the Floss, Jane Eyre (Ambassadors & tour); Anna Karenina (Tricycle & tour); The Tempest (tour); Great Expectations (Traverse); The Nose (Nottingham); The Cabinet of Dr. Caligari (Nottingham/Lyric); The Tempest, A Midsummer Night's Dream (Salisbury).

Television includes: Trial & Retribution, The Other Boleyn Girl, I Met Adolf Eichmann, Knit Your Own Karma, Anybody's Nightmare, Alive & Kicking, The Vice (Srs 2,3,& 4), Thursday the 12th, Great Expectations, Painted Lady, Big Day, 8 Hours From Paris, The Spy Who Caught a Cold, The Rat That Wrote, A Childhood, The Hidden Jews of Berlin, Remember The Family, The History of Tony Part, 3 Salons at the Seaside, Naked News.

John Sharian

For the Royal Court: Faith, The One You Love. Other theatre includes: Action (Young Vic); A Streetcar Named Desire, All My Sons, Lone Star & PVT Wars, The Life & Death of a Buffalo Soldier, The Hairy Ape (Bristol Old Vic); Life During Wartime (Lyric Studio); Macbeth (York Theatre); A Lie of the Mind (BAC); View From the Bridge (York Theatre Royal); Laundry Room at the Hotel Madrid (Gate Theatre); Small Craft Warnings (Manchester Library); Hamlet (Shaw Theatre); Entertaining Mr Sloane, Who's Afraid of Virginia Woolf, Safe Sex, The Importance of Being Earnest, Curse of the Starving Class, A Streetcar Named Desire (New Ehrlich Theatre, USA); As You Like It, American Buffalo, Servant of Two Masters, Getting Out (Kenyon Festival, USA); No End of Blame, The Castle (Playwrights' Platform USA), Two for the Seesaw, Harvey, Fifth of July (Tufts Arena Stage, USA); Macbeth (American Repertory Theatre); Baal, The Taming of the Shrew (Boston Stage Company).

Television includes: Sex Traffik, Small Potatoes, Chicken Ruin, Noel's House Party, Crocodile Shoes, Dead Men's Tales, Red Dwarf, Where in the World is Carmen Sandiego?

Film includes: Jason & the Argonauts, Do Not Disturb, Fortress 2, New World Disorder, 24 Hours in London, Saving Private Ryan, Lost in Space, Fifth Element, Death Machine, Two Sane Men, Romasanta, The Machinist.

Radio includes: Titanic Enquiries, Man of All Work.

Luke Wilson (assistant designer)

For the Royal Court: Terrorism. Other theatre includes: The Goat or Who is Sylvia? (Almeida); The Master Builder (Albery). Opera includes: Götterdämmerung (Scottish Opera/Edinburgh Festival.

Film includes: The Dance of Shiva, Ghosthunter. Luke has worked with Alison Chitty, Es Devlin and Jessica Curtis.

THE ENGLISH STAGE COMPANY AT THE ROYAL COURT

The English Stage Company at the Royal Court opened in 1956 as a subsidised theatre producing new British plays, international plays and some classical revivals.

The first artistic director George Devine aimed to create a writers' theatre, 'a place where the dramatist is acknowledged as the fundamental creative force in the theatre and where the play is more important than the actors, the director, the designer'. The urgent need was to find a contemporary style in which the play, the acting, direction and design are all combined. He believed that 'the battle will be a long one to continue to create the right conditions for writers to work in'.

Devine aimed to discover 'hard-hitting, uncompromising writers whose plays are stimulating, provocative and exciting'. The Royal Court production of John Osborne's Look Back in Anger in May 1956 is now seen as the decisive starting point of modern British drama and the policy created a new generation of British playwrights. The first wave included John Osborne, Arnold Wesker, John Arden, Ann Jellicoe, N F Simpson and Edward Bond. Early seasons included new international plays by Bertolt Brecht, Eugène Ionesco, Samuel Beckett, Jean-Paul Sartre and Marguerite Duras.

The theatre started with the 400-seat proscenium arch Theatre Downstairs, and then in 1969 opened a second theatre, the 60-seat studio Theatre Upstairs. Some productions transfer to the West End, such as Terry Johnson's Hitchcock Blonde, Caryl Churchill's Far Away, Conor McPherson's The Weir, Kevin Elyot's Mouth to Mouth and My Night With Reg. The Royal Court also co-produces plays which have transferred to the West End or toured internationally, such as Sebastian Barry's The Steward of Christendom and Mark Ravenhill's Shopping and Fucking (with Out of Joint), Martin McDonagh's The Beauty Queen of Leenane (with Druid Theatre Company), Ayub Khan-Din's East is East (with Tamasha Theatre Company, and now a feature film).

Since 1994 the Royal Court's artistic policy has again been vigorously directed to finding and producing a new generation of playwrights. The writers include Joe Penhall, Rebecca Prichard, Michael Wynne, Nick Grosso, Judy Upton, Meredith Oakes, Sarah Kane, Anthony Neilson, Judith Johnson, James Stock, Jez Butterworth, Marina Carr, Phyllis Nagy, Simon Block, Martin McDonagh, Mark Ravenhill, Ayub Khan-Din, Tamantha Hammerschlag, Jess Walters, Ché Walker, Conor McPherson, Simon

photo: Andy Chopping

Stephens, Richard Bean, Roy Williams, Gary Mitchell, Mick Mahoney, Rebecca Gilman, Christopher Shinn, Kia Corthron, David Gieselmann, Marius von Mayenburg, David Eldridge, Leo Butler, Zinnie Harris, Grae Cleugh, Roland Schimmelpfennig, DeObia Oparei, Vassily Sigarev, the Presnyakov Brothers and Lucy Prebble. This expanded programme of new plays has been made possible through the support of A.S.K Theater Projects and the Skirball Foundation, the Jerwood Charitable Foundation, the American Friends of the Royal Court Theatre and many in association with the Royal National Theatre Studio.

In recent years there have been record-breaking productions at the box office, with capacity houses for Roy Williams' Fallout, Terry Johnson's Hitchcock Blonde, Caryl Churchill's A Number, Jez Butterworth's The Night Heron, Rebecca Gilman's Boy Gets Girl, Kevin Elyot's Mouth to Mouth, David Hare's My Zinc Bed and Conor McPherson's The Weir, which transferred to the West End in October 1998 and ran for nearly two years at the Duke of York's Theatre.

The newly refurbished theatre in Sloane Square opened in February 2000, with a policy still inspired by the first artistic director George Devine. The Royal Court is an international theatre for new plays and new playwrights, and the work shapes contemporary drama in Britain and overseas.

AWARDS FOR
THE ROYAL COURT

Jez Butterworth won the 1995 George Devine Award, the Writers' Guild New Writer of the Year Award, the Evening Standard Award for Most Promising Playwright and the Olivier Award for Best Comedy for Mojo.

The Royal Court was the overall winner of the 1995 Prudential Award for the Arts for creativity, excellence, innovation and accessibility. The Royal Court Theatre Upstairs won the 1995 Peter Brook Empty Space Award for innovation and excellence in theatre.

Michael Wynne won the 1996 Meyer-Whitworth Award for The Knocky. Martin McDonagh won the 1996 George Devine Award, the 1996 Writers' Guild Best Fringe Play Award, the 1996 Critics' Circle Award and the 1996 Evening Standard Award for Most Promising Playwright for The Beauty Queen of Leenane. Marina Carr won the 19th Susan Smith Blackburn Prize (1996/7) for Portia Coughlan. Conor McPherson won the 1997 George Devine Award, the 1997 Critics' Circle Award and the 1997 Evening Standard Award for Most Promising Playwright for The Weir. Ayub Khan-Din won the 1997 Writers' Guild Awards for Best West End Play and Writers' Guild New Writer of the Year and the 1996 John Whiting Award for East is East (co-production with Tamasha).

At the 1998 Tony Awards, Martin McDonagh's The Beauty Queen of Leenane (co-production with Druid Theatre Company) won four awards including Garry Hynes for Best Director and was nominated for a further two. Eugene Ionesco's The Chairs (co-production with Theatre de Complicite) was nominated for six Tony awards. David Hare won the 1998 Time Out Live Award for Outstanding Achievement and six awards in New York including the Drama League, Drama Desk and New York Critics Circle Award for Via Dolorosa. Sarah Kane won the 1998 Arts Foundation Fellowship in Playwriting. Rebecca Prichard won the 1998 Critics' Circle Award for Most Promising Playwright for Yard Gal (co-production with Clean Break).

Conor McPherson won the 1999 Olivier Award for Best New Play for The Weir. The Royal Court won the 1999 ITI Award for Excellence in International Theatre. Sarah Kane's Cleansed was judged Best Foreign Language Play in 1999 by Theater Heute in Germany. Gary Mitchell won the 1999 Pearson Best Play Award for Trust. Rebecca Gilman was joint winner of the 1999 George Devine Award and won the 1999 Evening Standard Award for Most Promising Playwright for The Glory of Living.

In 1999, the Royal Court won the European theatre prize New Theatrical Realities, presented at Taormina Arte in Sicily, for its efforts in recent years in discovering and producing the work of young British dramatists.

Roy Williams and Gary Mitchell were joint winners of the George Devine Award 2000 for Most Promising Playwright for Lift Off and The Force of Change respectively. At the Barclays Theatre Awards 2000 presented by the TMA, Richard Wilson won the Best Director Award for David Gieselmann's Mr Kolpert and Jeremy Herbert won the Best Designer Award for Sarah Kane's 4.48 Psychosis. Gary Mitchell won the Evening Standard's Charles Wintour Award 2000 for Most Promising Playwright for The Force of Change. Stephen Jeffreys' I Just Stopped by to See The Man won an AT&T: On Stage Award 2000.

David Eldridge's Under the Blue Sky won the Time Out Live Award 2001 for Best New Play in the West End. Leo Butler won the George Devine Award 2001 for Most Promising Playwright for Redundant. Roy Williams won the Evening Standard's Charles Wintour Award 2001 for Most Promising Playwright for Clubland. Grae Cleugh won the 2001 Olivier Award for Most Promising Playwright for Fucking Games. Richard Bean was joint winner of the George Devine Award 2002 for Most Promising Playwright for Under the Whaleback. Caryl Churchill won the 2002 Evening Standard Award for Best New Play for A Number. Vassily Sigarev won the 2002 Evening Standard Charles Wintour Award for Most Promising Playwright for Plasticine. Ian MacNeil won the 2002 Evening Standard Award for Best Design for A Number and Plasticine. Peter Gill won the 2002 Critics' Circle Award for Best New Play for The York Realist (English Touring Theatre). Ché Walker won the 2003 George Devine Award for Most Promising Playwright for Flesh Wound. Lucy Prebble won the 2003 Critics' Circle Award for Most Promising Playwright.

ROYAL COURT BOOKSHOP

The bookshop offers a wide range of playtexts and theatre books, with over 1,000 titles. Located in the downstairs Bar and Food area, the bookshop is open Monday to Saturday, afternoons and evenings.

Many Royal Court playtexts are available for just £2 including works by Harold Pinter, Caryl Churchill, Rebecca Gilman, Martin Crimp, Sarah Kane, Conor McPherson, Ayub Khan-Din, Timberlake Wertenbaker and Roy Williams.

For information on titles and special events, Email: bookshop@royalcourttheatre.com
Tel: 020 7565 5024

Association of
London Government

Rebecca Gilman
The Sweetest Swing in Baseball

ff

faber and faber

First published in 2004
by Faber and Faber Limited
3 Queen Square London WC1N 3AU

Typeset by Country Setting, Kingsdown, Kent CT14 8ES
Printed in England by Mackays of Chatham plc, Chatham, Kent

A CIP record for this book
is available from the British Library

ISBN 0-571-22476-8

2 4 6 8 10 9 7 5 3 1

Characters

Dana, thirty-eight

Roy/Gary, forty

Rhonda/Dr Gilbert, forty

Brian/Michael, twenty-eight

Erica/Dr Stanton, forty-five

Place
Dana's studio, a gallery, and a mental hospital
in and near a large city.

Time
The present.

Notes
When Dana is being Darryl, she doesn't imitate him
or try to talk like an African-American. Her language
may be a little bit looser but she is essentially herself.

The character of Gary should not be played as a psycho
à la Hannibal Lector or any other 'psycho' types.
He is more of a hard-boiled crank. Imagine an actor
you might cast in *The Front Page*.

Sets and costumes should be very minimal. Dana can
wear the same costume for the entire play (black slacks
and a white T-shirt) and it can be dressed up or down
with accessories. She can make her changes on stage
as the scenery changes.

THE SWEETEST SWING IN BASEBALL

*The playscript that follows was correct
at the time of going to press, but may
have changed during rehearsals*

Act One

SCENE ONE

At rise: Dana's apartment. She is barefoot, wearing a white T-shirt and black slacks. She stands in front of an easel, staring at a painting. Whatever she is looking at, she is not happy with it. Paints and brushes are scattered on an old steamer trunk by her side. A boom box, covered in paint, plays classical music softly.

Keys in the door. Roy enters, wearing a black leather jacket and a black Homburg. He's been out drinking but he's not drunk, just loose. He sees Dana and looks tired.

Roy You still at it?

Dana Yes.

Roy How's it going?

Dana I don't know.

Roy walks up and looks at the canvas.

Could you not look over my shoulder?

Roy Sorry. (*He moves off.*) Did you start over?

Dana Yes.

Roy What was wrong with it?

Dana It was bullshit. It was like some cartoon fish tank or something. Did you see the blues?

Roy I thought they were nice.

Dana It looked like a giant bottle of Windex.

Roy Why don't you take a break?

Dana I can't.

Roy Well, maybe you think you can't, but if you took a break you could come back to it fresh tomorrow. And then you wouldn't have wasted all this time painting something you're just going to paint over again.

Dana Okay, that sounds like a good idea? But I have a show next week.

Roy I know.

Dana I have an opening on Friday and the postcards are out and people are coming and I don't want to show them a big empty room, if that's okay.

Roy All right. But it's past midnight.

Dana So?

Roy Have you eaten?

Dana No.

Roy Can I at least make you something to eat?

Dana I'm not hungry.

Roy I'm starving.

Dana Then eat something.

Roy If I make something, will you eat it?

Dana There's no food. (*She looks at the painting.*)

Roy It's going to be okay.

Dana I don't know what the fuck I'm doing.

Roy You always say that and then it's okay.

Dana When do I say that?

Roy Every time you paint anything you tell me you don't know what the fuck you're doing, and then the whole thing turns out fine.

Dana Fine?

Roy Great.

Dana Great?

Roy Outstanding.

Dana shakes her head. She doesn't believe him.

Dana Where'd you go?

Roy To the Hop Leaf.

Dana Was there a band?

Roy No. Scott was there. We just drank.

Dana Was that Stacey woman there?

Roy No. Why?

Dana I don't know. I just thought I saw you sitting in her car.

Roy What?

Dana About ten minutes ago. I looked out the window. I thought I saw you sitting in her car, in the front seat of her car, making out. (*Beat.*) I thought it looked like the two of you were . . . making out.

Roy Huh.

Dana Huh. (*Beat.*) Are you waiting for something? Why don't you just leave? (*Beat.*)

Roy You've got the show . . .

Dana Right.

Roy You've really been crazy.

Dana Uh-huh.

Roy I thought . . . (*Small beat.*) It's not Stacey. I don't give a shit about Stacey.

Dana Then what is it?

Roy (*hard for him*) I don't know. I guess I didn't want to come home.

Dana Why not?

Roy Because. (*Small beat.*) I always thought this was where we'd go to get away from it all. But now the whole apartment is about you and your career and . . . I don't know. I used to have the kitchen but there's brushes soaking everywhere and what am I supposed to do? Just sit in the bedroom?

Dana So you don't want me to paint?

Roy Of course I want you to paint. But I also want you to be happy. Sometimes I wish we could just chuck the whole art thing and work at Starbucks or something.

Dana Great idea.

Roy Well I don't know. (*Small beat. Still hard*) Sometimes, I think I'd be happier if I was alone.

Dana (*quiet*) When do you think that?

Roy I don't know. Sometimes. When I walk down the street, I look at all the apartment buildings and I wonder what they're like inside. Sometimes I think about getting my own place. A little place. With hardwood floors.

Dana We have hardwood floors.

Roy It's not the floors I want. It's being alone. (*Small beat.*)

Dana What would you do?

Roy I don't know. Sit on the floor.

Dana Sit on the floor?

Roy I don't know. I just thought, for a while, I could sit on the floor, and eat saltines. Maybe I'd get a goldfish. Or a guitar. Something to keep me company. But, I'd be alone.

Dana Which is better than being with me.

Roy I think, maybe, sometimes. (*Beat.*) I'm just a boyfriend, you know? I'm not a . . . mental health professional or whatever. And I can joke around and watch you paint, but I can't seem to talk you out of whatever it is you're in and I wish you would go see that therapist again –

Dana She was useless.

Roy She was no Dr Russell, but who will be?

Dana She kept telling me to drink herbal tea. That was her solution to everything.

Roy Okay. But you have to find somebody, because I can't do it for you. Obviously. I wish I could, but I can't seem to.

Dana You couldn't even stay through the show?

Roy You asked me to stay through the summer. And I did. And last spring. I stayed through that, too. And I was going to stay through the show, but it's October and . . . I'm making out with Stacey Edwards and I'm forty years old and what the fuck am I doing that for? That's not something I do.

Dana So Stacey Edwards is my fault?

Roy No. But . . .

Dana I make you crazy.

Roy doesn't answer. Pause. They stand. Then Dana picks up a brush to paint.

I make you crazy.

Roy No. It's just been hard is all.

Dana It's okay.

Roy Don't say it's okay.

Dana It's okay.

Roy I'm not disappearing on you. I'll be here if you need me.

Dana It's okay. The paintings are almost finished.

Roy Dana.

Dana They're probably better than I think.

Blackout.

SCENE TWO

In a corner of the gallery at Dana's opening. She is standing in gallery lighting in front of a wall that has 'Dana Fielding' painted on it in large letters and then some text that she is blocking. She wears a nicer shirt over the T-shirt, the same slacks and a pair of sandals. The sounds of an opening – people talking, laughing – surround her. Erica, an assistant at the gallery, stands with her. They are both drinking white wine from plastic cups.

Dana (*looks around*) Nobody's buying anything.

Erica People are more cautious. With the economy.

Dana I'm a fucking freak.

Erica Stop it. The paintings are great. They remind me of when I was a kid? In Utah? At night the colour of the desert was that sort of purple black. But you had to look to really see it. To see that it wasn't just black. (*Looks.*) They're really beautiful.

Dana (*cheered*) I'm glad you like them.

Erica The shading is so subtle.

Rhonda, the gallery owner, joins them.

Dana How's it going?

Rhonda Good, good.

Erica It's going great.

Rhonda Whatever happens, Dana, I want you to know I'm really proud we're showing your work. We all feel that way.

Erica We do.

Rhonda Whether the critics like it or not or whether anything sells isn't important. What's important is that the gallery is proud of the work we show. (*Small beat.*)

Dana It's totally bombing, isn't it?

Rhonda No.

Dana The show sucks. Everybody hates it.

Rhonda You're overstating it.

Erica I love them.

Dana You have to love them, you're my dealer.

Erica (*nervous laugh*) Rhonda's your dealer. I'm just a dealer in training.

Rhonda When Erica has her own gallery, she can be your dealer.

Dana I wasn't saying . . .

Rhonda No, no. I expect her to steal you away from me. After all, she did discover you.

Erica (*laughs*) It's not a plan or anything.

Rhonda But you won't be happy being my assistant for ever. Who would?

Erica I would.

Rhonda (*to Dana*) She's so loyal, but I keep telling her, don't be shy. When the moment's right, strike out on your own. You only need one really good artist to do it.

Erica Rhonda started out with Karina Novel.

Rhonda Who's still a hard sell.

Dana (*flat*) That rhymes. (*Beat.*)

Rhonda Dana, it's complicated work.

Erica People will have to wait for the critics to explain it. Then they'll love it.

Dana Who's here?

Rhonda Carl Jaffe.

Dana God.

Erica Now, your last show, you thought you got such a bad review from him and then I had fifteen people congratulate me on that review.

Dana He did not say a single positive thing about my work.

Erica He was very respectful.

Dana He called me opportunistic and evacuated. (*Small beat.*)

Rhonda Rachel Taylor is here. I ran into her last week at some benefit, and she said she's really been looking forward to this.

Dana nods, unconvinced.

You know, if you do work that's inaccessible, you're not going to get the sort of unqualified response you've had in the past. Which is a choice you've made, isn't it?

Dana I guess.

Rhonda You're making everybody nervous, though, standing here in the corner. You should talk to people. (*She exits.*)

Dana Why would I *choose* to be inaccessible?

Erica Shit just flows from her mouth.

Dana She wants you to steal me away so she won't have to deal with me any more.

Erica That's not true.

Dana I don't think she wants to include me in the biennial.

Erica (*worried*) Why do you say that?

Dana She already said something about not having the space to have as many artists and since I already had the solo show . . .

Erica She did?

Dana She'd want something new. They always want something new.

Erica So do something new.

Dana I don't have any ideas. (*indicating the paintings*) I pulled these out of my ass.

Erica You did not.

Dana I don't even know if they're ready to show. (*Small beat. She looks at the paintings.*) I don't know if I'm proud of them.

   Erica doesn't answer. Beat.

Erica Where's Roy?

Dana He left.

Erica Oh, I'm sorry I missed him.

Dana No, he wasn't here. He left me. He moved out.

Erica Oh God, Dana. I'm sorry.

Dana He said he would rather sit on the floor in an empty apartment than be with me.

Erica I'm sure he didn't say that.

Dana Yes he did.

Erica Well that was a stupid thing to say. You don't need that. You don't need that in your life. (*Beat.*) How are things going with your new therapist?

Dana I stopped seeing her.

Erica Why?

Dana She didn't believe anything I told her. Just factual things, like about how my dad died. I said he died of pneumonia and she said, '*Pneumonia*?' I was like, 'Yeah, people die of pneumonia. I can get you the death certificate if you don't believe me.'

Erica Do you think you could find somebody else?

Dana I had somebody else. I had Dr Russell, but she died.

Erica I know.

Dana I loved her. She didn't just tell me how special I was. She tried to help me figure out ways to fix things. These other people are clueless. I'm on my fifth one already.

Erica Maybe you're too picky.

Dana Dr Rosenberg fell asleep while I was talking to her.

Erica Well, we have to find someone because I'm worried about you. (*Hates to say it.*) I do think your work is suffering.

Dana (*stifling the yell*) Oh my God, you don't think I know that?

Erica reaches out to take her hand when Brian enters. He is very hip.

Brian Hey. Congratulations.

Dana (*quickly composing herself*) Hi, Brian. Thanks for coming.

Erica (*to Dana*) I'll get you some more wine. (*Erica exits.*)

Brian (*looks towards the paintings*) They're really intriguing.

Dana Thanks.

Brian I thought I read in some interview that you were going to show that series on iconic portraiture.

Dana I don't think I called it 'iconic portraiture'. It was more just . . . portraits.

Brian Did you change your mind?

Dana I didn't finish them. I . . . they were more involved than I thought they'd be? And I was committed to these dates so I did these instead.

Brian Well, these are really intriguing.

Dana Thanks. (*Beat. Trying to be nice*) So what's going on with you?

Brian Well. I just got this inter-media arts grant for an installation I'm doing at CAM in March.

Dana Congratulations.

Brian (*grins*) And then I've got a show at Riley Kuhn. In December.

Dana No way! That's great.

Brian I'm really pleased.

Dana You should be. That's a huge deal.

Brian Yeah. I really wanted it. (*Small beat.*) I guess I should thank you for recommending me. Bill Riley said you sent him over to Presence, to see my stuff in that loan show.

Dana Oh, it was my pleasure. I thought it was really good work.

Brian Yeah, he totally dug it.

Dana Good.

> *Pause. He doesn't actually thank her. They drink their wine.*

Brian So what's next for you?

Dana I don't have anything lined up right now.

Brian You'll be in the biennial, though.

Dana Should be, yeah.

Brian Well, I can't wait to see that other series. The portraits. Let me know when they're finished.

Dana I will.

Brian And come see my show.

Dana I will.

> *He exits. Dana stands alone for a moment. Rhonda enters.*

Rhonda You know the people who get it really do get it.

Dana Oh yeah?

Rhonda It's just . . . I don't know. Take this for what it's worth, okay? But I was just talking to Rachel Taylor and she said an interesting thing, which is you're much more technically proficient than you used to be. I mean just craft-wise, you're among some of the best out there. But, it's almost funny, it's like what people liked about your earlier work was its messiness, you know? I told her, when I saw some of these paintings in their early stages in your studio, there was a rawness to them, and I think I suggested at the time, that they needed to be explained –

Dana You did.

Rhonda And the technical changes were really smart, really smart. But now I'm wondering if maybe I was wrong. Because now I'm missing that visceral quality they had. It'd be great if you could go back and capture that, but I imagine that's impossible. Especially when you've worked so hard to lose it. (*Small beat.*) I don't know. It's a challenge, isn't it?

Erica enters with another glass of wine.

(*to Erica*) You should come meet Tamara Young.

Erica Go ahead. I'll catch up.

Rhonda exits. Erica hands the wine to Dana.

What do you want to do?

Dana shrugs. She might cry.

Do you want to take some time off?

Dana I don't know.

Erica What if you just took some time off and you spent some time by yourself, and you stopped listening to these assholes? (*Beat.*) Dana?

Blackout.

SCENE THREE

*The occupational therapy room at a psychiatric hospital.
At a table sit Dana, Gary and Michael. Gary is a regular-
looking man in his forties, wearing hospital scrubs and
a pocket T-shirt and slippers. Michael is thin, early
twenties, looks terrible. His hair is a mess and his hands
shake. Dana is wearing the white T-shirt, black slacks
and flip-flops. She looks rumpled, her hair pulled back.
Each of her wrists is wrapped in a clean white bandage,
five inches wide. Gary is drawing with a charcoal pencil.
Michael stares into space, an untouched pencil and paper
in front of him. Dana sits in the middle with a pile of
modelling clay which she is simply mashing between
her fingers.*

    *Gary, who has been working intently on his drawing,
glances over at his two companions.*

Gary The name of the game is occupational therapy.

    Dana looks at him.

You should try making something.

    *Dana looks at the clay, then she takes what's in her
    hand and rolls it into a ball. She puts the ball on the
    table. She and Gary look at it.*

That's terrific. A ball.

    Dana looks at it.

Dana It's a cannonball, actually.

Gary Suit yourself. But the time goes faster if you make
something. (*Gary shows her his drawing.*) Here's what
I've been working on.

Dana (*eyes widen*) Wow.

Gary I know. The verisimilitude, right?

Dana Yeah.

Gary senses something in the way she's looking at it.

Gary What?

Dana Nothing. It's great.

Gary It's not finished.

Dana I know.

Gary This guy's arm is too long.

Dana It's a little long.

Gary He looks like a fucking ape. (*Gary pulls the drawing back.*)

Dana I didn't say that. It's just a little long.

Gary starts erasing the line, frustrated. Dana hesitates, but then jumps in.

Have you tried drawing the negative space? Instead of the object itself?

Gary The what?

Dana The negative space is the space around the object. (*indicating on the drawing*) Like, there's a triangle here, between this guy's arm . . . and this guy's neck . . . and the knife blade. That's the negative space. (*She turns to Michael.*) Can I borrow your pencil?

Michael Sure.

She uses Michael to illustrate her point. Using his pencil as a 'knife', she mimes bringing her hand down toward Michael's jugular. Then with her other hand, she traces the triangle she's made. Michael doesn't react during any of this.

Dana See if he was on the ground and I'm on top of him bringing the knife into his neck . . . see how there's more length to the – what is it? – a carving knife?

Gary Yeah.

Dana So try lengthening that side of the triangle and you'll fix the length of the arm.

Gary Uh-huh.

Dana Do you want me to show you?

Gary Yeah.

He pushes the paper over and she draws for him. Michael looks.

Michael Why is that guy's shadow all gloopy like that?

Gary It's not a shadow, it's blood.

Michael Oh.

Dana Then make it reflective – where's your light source? Is this a lamp post?

Gary Yeah.

Dana Then your primary shadow would be here and the light would hit here. You can lighten towards the centre using your kneaded eraser . . . (*She picks up the eraser.*) Then – well, I don't have a blending pencil, but you can use your finger to soften that edge of the blood pool –

She works. Gary and Michael watch.

Gary You're getting crap all over your bandages.

Dana What?

Gary You're turning your bandages black.

Dana stops, looks at her bandages, now covered in charcoal.

You still got the stitches in?

Dana Yeah.

Gary Did you cut horizontally or vertically?

Dana Vertically.

Gary See, I don't get that. You're worried about slicing your tendons? What does it matter? Presumably you're going to be dead, right?

Dana I was trying to cut along the artery.

Gary But I bet you're glad you've got your tendons now, right?

Dana I guess.

Gary Where'd you do it?

Dana In my bathroom.

Gary Who found you?

Dana My ex-boyfriend.

Gary You were expecting him to come by?

Dana No. (*Beat.*) I told everybody I was going out of town. That's why he came over. Because he thought I wouldn't be there.

Gary I'd use a gun. That way you'd know for sure.

Michael I'd jump.

Dana I used an X-Acto knife. (*Beat.*) They're very precise.

Gary If you really wanted to die, you'd be dead. You just wanted attention.

Dana No, I didn't, I wanted to die. I would have too, if my ex-boyfriend hadn't come by to get his stupid Nina Simone CDs.

Gary How long you been here?

Dana I got here last night.

Gary Who's your doctor?

Dana I don't know. Dr Stanton admitted me but I haven't met her yet.

Gary How'd you get in her unit?

Dana I don't know.

Gary It's hard to get in Stanton's unit. You must know somebody.

Dana I don't know anybody. My dealer arranged it while I was in the hospital.

Michael Your dealer?

Dana My art dealer. Erica. (*Small beat.*)

Michael I'm in rehab. It's my second time.

Gary You a crack addict?

Michael I'm an alcoholic.

Gary For how long?

Michael Since I was fifteen. My dad's an alcoholic, not in recovery.

Gary I've never touched alcohol in my life. The day I end up a gutless alcoholic is the day I want somebody to put a bullet in my brain.

Small beat. Michael sits up.

Michael So are you a psycho, or what?

Gary Yeah. I tried to kill a guy.

Both Dana and Michael sit back.

You may have heard of him. Kevin Bridges.

Michael Oh my God. You're that guy. Who tried to kill Kevin Bridges.

Gary Yeah.

Michael You're that crazy stalker guy. I heard you were in here.

Gary Yeah.

Michael Now, let me get this straight. Do you think you're Kevin Bridges?

Gary No. I just want to kill him.

Michael Why?

Gary Because he is the seat of all evil.

Dana Kevin Bridges is that newscaster, right?

Michael He's an anchor on CNN.

Gary He uses his position in the media to disseminate evil.

Dana (*to Gary*) Shouldn't you be in jail or something?

Gary I was remanded to the Psych Ward. I'm insane.

They look at him.

I'm on a lot of medication.

Michael Oh.

Gary Normally I'm over in the East Wing, but if your doc can prove you're no immediate harm to yourself or others then you get privileges. I get to come in here and on Sundays I get to swim.

Michael You get to swim? I don't get to swim.

Gary Swimming's a privilege. You have to earn it.

Dana (*to Gary*) So you're not dangerous?

Gary Only to Kevin Bridges. (*Beat. Gary regards Dana.*) You don't seem depressed enough. To try to kill yourself.

Dana How the hell would you know?

Gary Back off. It's a compliment. You seem normal.

They go back to their work.

Yeah, you'll be out of here by next week.

Dana Next week?

Gary Who's your carrier?

Dana My what?

Gary Insurance.

Dana Golden Rule.

Gary Ten days is all they'll cover.

Dana Ten days?

Michael You get twenty-eight for rehab.

Gary I got life.

Dana is preoccupied.

What's the matter? You afraid to go home?

Dana No.

Gary Afraid you'll kill yourself?

Dana No.

Gary Why are you afraid of it, if it's what you want to do?

Dana (*snaps*) I'm not afraid. Okay?

Michael Leave her alone.

Gary Okay.

Dana picks up a piece of clay and slowly rolls it into a ball.

So why'd you do it?

Blackout.

SCENE FOUR

Dr Gilbert's office. She sits in an ugly leather chair and holds a file. She is a good, efficient therapist.
Dana sits across from her in a plain chair. She is dressed as before.

Gilbert It looks like Dr Stanton shared a practice with your former therapist . . .

Dana Dr Russell. She died.

Gilbert That's why Dr Stanton brought you in. She wanted to make sure you were taken care of.

Dana Oh. I didn't know how I got here.

Gilbert You're lucky we had a spot. There's a waiting list. (*Opens the file.*) So I'm sorry no one could meet with you yesterday. But I guess you've sort of gotten the lay of the land. Dr Stanton's unit is very small – only six patients – so we do share the common areas of the hospital with other units. But you'll only see me for therapy.

Dana I won't see Dr Stanton?

Gilbert She has a full load. (*Smiles.*) But I've been working with Dr Stanton for twelve years, so I think I'm qualified to treat you.

Dana Oh, sure, of course.

Gilbert I understand you've already met Gary Richards.

Dana He's the psycho?

Gilbert He's our most notorious patient. As long as he's on medication he's stable. But I'd give him a wide berth anyway. Technically, he is a sociopath.

Dana He did seem kind of cranky.

Gilbert (*looks at her file*) Okay. Now, are you on any medications right now?

Dana No.

Gilbert And what about in the past?

Dana Just birth-control pills.

Gilbert You've never been on any anti-depressants?

Dana No.

Gilbert Was that Dr Russell's decision, or . . .?

Dana That was my decision.

Gilbert And why is that?

Dana I guess I really feel like I didn't want to take something that would change my personality. I feel like your brain determines your identity, and when you mess with the chemistry in your brain, you fundamentally mess with who you are. And if I mess with who I am then I mess with my painting.

Gilbert I understand what you're saying, but the anti-depressants that are around today don't alter your personality. They just work to correct a chemical imbalance in your brain. Which is often the cause of depression.

Dana It's not always the cause of depression.

Gilbert No. Some depressions are situational. If there's a death in the family, or some sort of traumatic experience –

Dana Or your life just sucks.

Gilbert But often life feels like it . . . sucks, because of this chemical imbalance. Does that make sense?

Dana Yeah, except my life does suck. You know? My parents died, my boyfriend left me. My career's a joke.

Gilbert Let's back up. When did your parents die?

Dana My dad died when I was twenty-one. Of pneumonia.

She gives a small beat to see how this registers. Gilbert nods.

And my mom died five years ago from cancer.

Gilbert Is that when you started seeing Dr Russell?

Dana Yeah. You know, I went through all of this with her. About my parents.

Gilbert Was there a lot to work on?

Dana No. (*Beat.*) I miss them. Is all.

Gilbert (*smiles*) For my benefit, since we don't know each other, could you tell me something about them? A thumbnail sketch, as it were?

Dana Okay. My dad was an attorney. But he was also a farmer – sort of a gentlemen farmer. As it were. But he didn't know anything about livestock or crops? So he lost a lot of money on it. But my mom didn't seem to mind because he enjoyed it so much, how could you be mad at him? And she was a nurse. (*Small beat.*)

Gilbert Okay. Do you have any siblings?

Dana No.

Gilbert Then you've been on your own for a while now.

Dana I had Roy. My boyfriend? But you know, he dumped me.

Gilbert When was that?

Dana A couple of months ago. We lived together.

Gilbert Was this sudden?

Dana Not really. I knew he wasn't happy? But I kept begging him to stay, because I was so freaked out. Which is pathetic because we weren't getting along. I just didn't want to be by myself.

Gilbert Why weren't you getting along?

Dana Well, we did when we first met. I thought he was really funny and he makes these mixed-media boxes with little twigs and rocks that he collects and I thought they were really interesting. But when we moved in together he started walking around the apartment naked. Or sometimes he would walk around naked except for a hat. He had this idea like our place was this sanctuary where we could be all domestic together and bake bread and – (*Stops.*) I never said anything about baking bread. I never made bread in my life. And then he was always changing his facial hair. Long sideburns. Goatee. One of those soul patch things. I was like, 'Give me a break and stop reinventing yourself every five minutes.' So he went off and made out with Stacey Edwards, who is this chick who – about five hundred years ago? – was in a Smiths video. In like, 1985 or something, but everybody still thinks she's really hot. But it's not 1985 and we're not in high school. So I said, 'Go ahead and leave already.' And he did.

Gilbert And why were you freaked out?

Dana You pay attention?

Gilbert I try.

Dana I had a solo show a couple of months ago at Rhonda Block – and it was a ton of pressure –

Gilbert I'm sorry, is this a gallery?

Dana Yeah, Rhonda's my dealer. She shows like . . . well, famous artists that nobody's ever heard of. She's a huge deal.

Gilbert And you had a show there. That's great.

Dana It tanked.

Gilbert What?

Dana It completely tanked. I got creamed in the press and I didn't sell crap and it was a train wreck.

Gilbert Are you exaggerating?

Dana No. It was awful. My phone stopped ringing. Even Erica stopped calling me.

Gilbert Who's Erica?

Dana She's Rhonda's assistant. She discovered me, or whatever. (*Small beat.*) It's a bad sign when Erica won't call me.

Gilbert Maybe she thought you needed some space.

Dana Maybe she thinks she hitched her wagon to the wrong horse.

Gilbert But this was only one show.

Dana No. It's been a steady decline. My first show, everybody was all hyped up. They were all saying I was like, the new vision of a new generation or something, but with every other show since then everybody's been acting like I'm never going to live up to that original potential. (*Small beat.*) I tried to stop worrying about it. Like I tried to get back to doing art for art's sake, or whatever, just painting to please myself. And I stopped reading any reviews, because they were completely fucking with my head. Like a while back, this woman

Margarite Mosely said that I relied too heavily on reds, I had a preponderance of reds in my canvases and so the next time I went to paint, all of a sudden I had a colour wheel in my head and it was like the entire spectrum was suddenly off limits. You know? Then I'd put down a yellow and it started looking too orange or the blues were too violet and I just got all freaked out and everything just turned out black. Because this one idiot didn't like my reds.

Gilbert (*nods*) Which is one thing about depression. It's sort of a black hole, in that it can colour everything around us.

Dana No pun intended.

Gilbert Actually, no. No pun intended. It's a black hole. So maybe you get this review and then suddenly it's all you can think about – it's huge. When in reality, it's not that huge, is it?

Dana (*unsure*) No.

Gilbert Which is the only reason I suggested we look at medication. It's not a happy pill, or anything, but it can help to increase a natural chemical in your brain –

Dana You're talking about seratonin re-uptake inhibitors. (*Tiny beat.*) I've done some research.

Gilbert Then you should know that all the medication does is, it pulls you up to a level where you can become more resilient. So that these upsets don't seem quite so monumental.

Dana Or it makes you able to tolerate an intolerable situation. So instead of fixing the root cause of the illness, you just learn to live with the symptoms. (*Small beat.*)

Gilbert All right, let's look at this a different way. If you had a problem with your eyes, for example, you'd get corrective lenses –

Dana (*getting angry*) It's not the same.

Gilbert But it may be.

Dana No. There's no problem with the way I see things. The way I see things is perfectly accurate. The problem is with the things I see.

Gilbert Okay. I don't want us to become focused solely on this issue. It's not the best use of our time right now.

Dana You're going to kick me out, aren't you?

Gilbert What?

Dana I heard my insurance will only pay for ten days.

Gilbert It depends on your progress –

Dana I'm self-employed, my insurance is the cheapest one. Golden Rule. I think it only covers if I get hit by a bus.

Gilbert (*small beat*) Then we'll continue therapy on an out-patient basis, if we have to. We're here to help you for as long as you need help.

Dana But it'd go a lot faster if I went on the drugs.

Gilbert I'm not implying that.

Dana You know, the thing about those stupid drugs is if I take them, that makes me the problem. But I'm not the problem.

Gilbert It was only a suggestion –

Dana I'm not trying to kill anybody or hurt anybody, all I'm trying to do is paint.

End of scene.

The common room. Uncomfortable chairs. Michael and Dana are watching TV. Michael looks more alert, less shaky. Dana has a book in her hand that she is not reading.

Michael Okay . . . (*He watches.*) That's the guy I like.

Dana What does the winner get?

Michael A recording contract.

Dana How do they pick?

Michael You call in and vote.

  They watch. A commercial comes on and Michael mutes it. Dana looks at her book.

Dana The nurse loaned me this romance novel but it's awful.

Michael Did you not bring any books?

Dana No.

Michael We've got a whole library over in rehab. But it's all twelve-step books. Or books by recovering addicts. (*Laughs.*) Half of them, you look at them and the people who wrote the book ended up dead from an overdose. They're really inspiring tales of sobriety.

Dana This is your second time here?

Michael Yeah.

Dana Did something happen . . . ?

Michael I went on a binge. I mean nothing happened to make me go on a binge, I just went on a binge. And I wasn't eating and my sodium levels went haywire. My

34

super found me in the lobby, I guess I was falling all over the place and I couldn't talk. He thought I had a brain tumor. But. No such luck.

Dana Don't say that.

Michael I'm not complaining. I'm alive. They're even holding my job for me.

Dana What do you do?

Michael I write code. For computers.

Dana So you have an actual skill.

Michael (*laughs*) Yeah.

> *Erica enters. She looks very nervous. She carries a small bag.*

Erica Dana?

Dana Oh, wow.

Erica Hey.

Dana I forgot you were coming.

Erica They said you gave permission.

Dana Yeah, I just – (*She looks at her wrist. She's not wearing a watch.*) I don't have a watch or anything. Is it Tuesday already?

Erica It's Wednesday.

Dana Right. I lost track of time. (*Looks around.*) Did they say where we should go?

Michael I'll leave.

Dana You're watching your show.

Michael I don't mind.

Dana (*to Erica*) This is my friend Michael.

Michael Hi.

Erica Hi.

Michael (*to Dana*) Come get me when you're through, okay? (*He exits.*)

Erica (*doesn't know where to start. Hands Dana the bag*) This is stupid but I brought you make-up.

Dana Make-up?

Erica I called and asked if I could bring anything, and they said a lot of women liked make-up. If you hadn't brought any in with you. When I packed your bag before, I didn't think to put any in. And I . . . the bathroom was kind of . . . I only packed your clothes.

Dana That's okay.

Erica So I brought some mascara and blush and foundation. I couldn't really remember if you wore anything or not. I know you're more of a 'natural look' kind of person. (*Beat.*) Roy wanted to know if he could come.

Dana No.

Erica He feels like you meant for him to find you.

Dana I didn't mean for anybody to find me.

Erica I know. (*Upset.*) You really really scared me.

Dana I'm sorry.

Erica I thought you were going to die. When I got to the hospital Roy was – your blood was on him and I thought you were dead.

Dana Why was my blood on him?

Erica He must have been holding you. (*Beat.*) We both . . . we felt terrible we didn't call you. I didn't call you for so long because I thought you wanted to be left alone. I thought I would leave you alone but I shouldn't have done that. I didn't know what was happening. And you never called me, so I didn't know.

Dana I didn't think anybody wanted to talk to me.

Erica But you can't go and kill yourself without even, you know, calling to see if maybe I could talk you out of it or something. It's not fair. You have to give people a chance to help you.

Dana I'm sorry.

Erica It's okay. You just scared me.

    They sit. Pause.

A lot of people have called. (*Laughs.*) Rhonda thinks she drove you to it.

Dana She kind of did.

Erica She still wants to work with you.

Dana (*laughs*) She probably wishes I was dead. Then she could have a retrospective. Double the prices. People really start to appreciate you when you're dead.

Erica People really *miss* you when you're dead. (*Beat.*) So tell me what they have you doing here. Have you seen Dr Stanton?

Dana No. I've been seeing this Dr Gilbert woman.

Erica Do you like her?

Dana She's okay. (*Beat.*)

Erica What else do you do?

Dana We have occupational therapy. We watch movies. Last night was Mexican night. They let us go in the kitchen and make tacos.

Erica Are you making some friends?

Dana There's this guy named Gary who's very interesting. He's . . . very interested in the news. (*Indicates.*) And Michael. I like Michael. He's not in my unit, though.

Erica Do you have a room-mate?

Dana Her name's Virginia. She never talks.

Erica Why doesn't she talk?

Dana She never talks and she never gets out of bed. I don't know what the deal is. I did ask her last night if she was hot – it was hot in our room – and she kind of grunted. So that seems promising. (*Beat.*) Dr Gilbert won't say for sure, but I think I can only stay a few more days. Because of my insurance. It's too expensive. It's a thousand dollars a day so I can't stay if the insurance won't pay.

Erica I wish I could help –

Dana I'm not asking you to pay.

Erica I could give you a couple of thousand but –

Dana I'm not asking you for money, Erica. (*Small beat.*) I don't suppose Rhonda would offer?

Erica doesn't answer.

No, I don't suppose she would.

Erica We'll figure something out.

Dana Dr Gilbert says she'll see me on an out-patient basis –

Erica Good.

Dana (*overlapping*) But I'm afraid if I go home, if I have to look at my studio with all that crap everywhere –

Erica I tried to clean it.

Dana And that bathroom –

Erica You painted on the walls, though. Should I paint over it?

Dana With those tiles, those little octagonal tiles. They're so hard not to stare at. I kind of got obsessed with them. But not in a good way. (*Laughs.*) There's that crack along the floor where the tiles to the left are slightly higher than the ones on the right? From there, I tried to count all the tiles but the rows are hard to keep straight and after a while, they kind of blurred together and I stopped seeing the grout. Just these octagons, fitting up against all these other octagons. I had this feeling like, if one of the octagons could just get free . . . If it could just get away from the other octagons everything would be okay, but . . . (*Laughs again.*) And then I thought, I'm lying on the bathroom floor. I don't know how I got *there*. (*Beat.*) It's a very cold floor. When you step out of the shower? It's very cold. (*Small beat.*) Virginia and I both have little stations here, in the bathroom, with a mirror and shelves on either side for our stuff. Then the dresser is built in under the mirror. It's maple. Maple is a nice, warm wood, I think.

Erica (*looks at her. Gentle*) You could put your make-up on one of the shelves.

Dana I could.

   They sit for a moment.

Is there anything in that portrait series you think you could sell?

Erica I don't know. You don't want to get overexposed, you know. It makes you a target.

Dana I tried to kill myself. I already feel like a target.

Erica I'm just not sure it's the best strategy right now.

Dana I don't want a strategy. I want to stay here.

Erica But I hate to sell things for less than their full value because you feel desperate.

Dana I don't care.

Erica I do, though, I'm thinking about your future.

Dana What future?

Erica Your future. Your career.

Dana I don't care about my career. Would you stop being my dealer for five seconds and just – (*Stops.*) Just sell the goddamn paintings. (*Beat.*)

Erica (*reluctantly*) I don't know if I can. A lot of people passed on the last show. (*Beat.*) And I'm not your dealer, I'm your friend.

    Pause. Dana takes this in.

Dana So . . . you don't want your fifty per cent any more?

    End of scene.

SCENE SIX

The occupational therapy room. Gary is still working on his drawing. Michael is flipping through a book and has another pile of books beside him. Dana has a child's box of watercolours and a styrofoam cup of water and is painting on a piece of butcher paper.

Gary If you want to stay you have to have a major diagnosis. Depression won't cut it.

Dana Like what?

Gary Paranoid schizophrenia. Multiple personality disorder. Manic depressive.

Dana I thought about trying to kill myself again –

Michael Dana.

Dana But how do I do it? There's nothing in my room. My room-mate's on a suicide watch –

Michael *You're* probably on a suicide watch.

Dana Whatever. But they won't even let me keep a blow dryer in the room. In case she wants to electrocute herself. I have to dry my hair at the nurses' station.

Gary You don't need a blow dryer. There's a million ways if you really want to. You could kill yourself with this pencil. Jab it right through your eyeball and into your brain.

Michael Could we not talk about this?

Gary But that's just a stop-gap measure anyway.

Michael Sticking a pencil in your brain?

Gary Trying to kill yourself. You just buy another ten days maybe. And unfortunately it's a catch-22 situation. The fact that you want to stay means you like the safety of the place, which means you have a healthy sense of self-preservation, which means you're not really suicidal, which means you're probably ready to go home.

Dana Great.

Michael Maybe it won't be so bad.

Dana I'm pretty sure it's going to be bad.

Beat. Michael looks at what she's painting. Trying to cheer her up:

Michael That's cool.

Dana This is a . . . it's a tern.

Gary A what?

Dana A tern? Like a gull, or a duck?

Gary (*looks*) I thought you were a famous artist.

Dana I don't normally paint terns. I just . . . it's actually, well, it's kind of stupid, but when I was a kid I drew my own comic strip? And these were the characters. (*Shrugs.*) But it's stupid.

Michael No it's not. Who are they?

Dana Well, this is CT. Contemplative Tern. He's like the mayor of the woodlands. Because he's so thoughtful. And this is Deluded Dan the Chipmunk Man. He's obese, but he thinks he's pleasantly plump. Then this is the Ghost Bison. He's haunted by visions of his decimated herd. And then this dot over here is a gnat. He just hangs around and says really smart things when nobody's expecting it.

Gary and Michael look at the comic.

Gary You should call him Erudite Gnat.

Dana That's kind of a mouthful.

Gary No more than Contemplative Tern.

Michael He has a point.

Dana Okay. Erudite Gnat. (*Beat.*) Anyway. I used to draw little adventures for them. I had completely forgotten about it but the paints reminded me.

Michael I wish I had known you when I was a kid. The kids I grew up with were complete jarheads. Creativity to them was blowing up a cat with a cherry bomb.

Dana All the kids I grew up with thought I was weird.

Gary You were.

Michael (*pushing the books forward, blocking off Gary*) So anyway, I brought you all these books from our library, but I guess you won't need them if you're leaving.

Dana I can still read a couple.

Michael I tried to pick good ones. Billy Carter? Remember him?

Dana Sure. Billy beer.

Michael I always felt sorry for him. Your brother's the president and you're, like, working in a feed store or something. (*picking up another book*) And this one's good. Darryl Strawberry, *Recovering Life*. Get it? *Recovering life*?

Gary She gets it.

Michael Two months after he wrote it he got arrested for possession.

Gary He was a bum.

Michael He had a hard life.

Gary What? Somebody paid him ten million dollars to play catch?

Michael He had a bad childhood. He didn't have any coping skills.

Gary He didn't run out routine grounders. Is what he didn't do. He was a drunk.

Michael Alcoholic.

Gary Call it what you want, it doesn't change anything. When you have talent like that and you waste it . . . ? (*Beat.*) When he was sober, he had a perfect swing. Perfect follow-through. Sweetest swing I ever saw.

Michael Yeah. (*Beat.*)

Gary So you a baseball fan?

Michael Yeah.

Gary I thought you were gay.

Michael The two are not mutually exclusive.

Gary I just never met a gay guy who was into sports. I've met a lot of gay guys who were drunks, though.

Michael Oh yeah? (*He pushes the books over to Dana.*) Anyway. Read what you can.

Dana Thanks. (*to Gary*) Could I fake one of those things? Like the paranoid schizophrenia?

Gary No way you can fake that. You thinking of faking something?

Dana I thought maybe if I had something more serious, they wouldn't send me home.

Gary Yeah, you're not the first one to think that. But it's too hard. These people are professionals.

Dana Then they should know not to send me home.

   Pause.

Gary You could maybe buy some time with something milder.

Michael People fake multiple personality disorders. Like Sybil.

Dana Sybil was a faker?

Michael I'm just saying, model yourself on Sybil.

Gary MPD's too hard. You could do like a Mark David Chapman maybe. He just thought he was John Lennon. Which is why he had to eliminate John Lennon. Because John Lennon was impersonating him, Mark David Chapman. Who was John Lennon.

Michael But you don't think you're Kevin Bridges.

Gary No. I explained that already.

Dana Did he walk around acting like John Lennon?

Gary He was too fucked up. It was sort of an internal thing. But when he bought the gun that he used to kill John Lennon, he signed the receipt 'John Lennon'.

Michael So are you trying to kill Kevin Bridges to impress somebody? Like what's-his-head did, with Jody Foster?

Gary No. I already told you why I want to kill him.

Michael But how is he evil, exactly?

Gary He's just very evil.

Michael Does he do evil things?

Gary Yes.

Michael Like what?

Gary He comes into my living room every night and talks down to me. Okay? That alone is reason enough to kill him. Plus he talks endlessly about the Middle East and Middle Eastern relations. Okay?

Michael I guess.

Dana Do I have to kill somebody, though? Because I really don't want to kill anybody.

Gary Not necessarily. But it should have a sort of scary edge to it, I think.

Michael I don't think it needs to be scary.

Gary It should stand out, though.

Michael (*to Dana*) Who are you going to be?

45

Dana I don't know.

Gary Don't pick some artist. Like don't suddenly become Picasso or something. That's way too obvious.

Dana Oh God. There's no way I'd be an artist.

What she's said hangs in the air for a moment. The other two look at her.

What? I want to be something good.

End of scene.

SCENE SEVEN

Dr Gilbert's office. Dana sits across from her.

Gilbert I think for the rest of this session, we should focus on what's going to happen when you leave tomorrow. These are simply strategies for getting through your days, at first.

Dana Okay.

Gilbert Now how long do you think it will take you to find a new place?

Dana I don't know. But Erica said I could stay with her if I didn't want to go home.

Gilbert Well it would be better if you didn't stay with Erica for too long, simply because we want to get you into a normal routine.

Dana Can I use the routine I have here? Because before I just slept. And ate toast. And went crazy.

Gilbert It's not a given that you'll go back to that.

Dana You're right. I probably won't sleep. Or eat. (*Beat.*)

Gilbert You know, these are the very kinds of problems that can be treated with medication –

Dana No.

Gilbert Disruptions in sleep patterns, loss of appetite, anxiety, these are easily treated symptoms.

Dana I told you, no.

Gilbert Couldn't you just agree to try it – if you don't like the way it makes you feel, we can take you off, or we can change medications.

Dana I can't.

Gilbert I'm not talking life-long meds –

Dana I can't, okay? I already explained that to you. (*Tiny beat.*) I have to be drug-free. I have to be drug-free because they come in and they test me. Every day, they come in and ask for a urine sample and I can't fuck with that. I gotta stay clean.

Gilbert (*not following*) Someone tests you?

Dana The commissioner's office. They send somebody in.

Gilbert What?

Dana Some dude. From the commissioner's office. He comes in and watches you piss in a cup. It's serious. Serious shit.

Gilbert What are you talking about?

Dana I'm saying, I'm not taking any drugs. I'm not taking any risks that it comes up something weird and they don't let me play.

Gilbert Play what?

Dana Baseball.

Gilbert You play baseball?

Dana (*laughs*) Fuck yeah I play baseball. (*Small beat. Not completely sure*) I'm the Straw.

Gilbert What?

Dana Darryl Strawberry? The Straw?

   Gilbert looks at her.

Are you okay?

Gilbert Dana, I –

Dana Who the hell's Dana?

Gilbert You.

Dana Nuh-uh.

Gilbert Yes.

Dana No way.

Gilbert Stop doing whatever you're doing.

Dana I'm just talking.

Gilbert But what are you talking about?

Dana I'm talking about, how all of baseball's looking at me, wondering, 'Is he coked up? Is he on the stuff? The crack? The crank? The . . . stuff?' It's sad, but I have to earn back their trust. Can I do it? I don't know. I'm scared. But fuck, who isn't?

Gilbert I'm scared right now.

Dana See? That's why you start shooting smack. (*Small beat.*) Although technically I'm not a heroin addict. I'm an alcoholic and I snort cocaine.

Gilbert No you don't.

Dana I don't now, but I did. Sister, did I ever. Which is why I have to say, thanks for the offer, Doc, but I can't put any drugs in this body.

Small beat. Gilbert isn't answering, so Dana goes ahead.

I have to protect it. So I can play, once again, for the New York Yankees. (*Beat.*)

Gilbert Dana –

Dana I don't know why you keep calling me Dana. My name's not Dana.

Gilbert Dana.

Dana Dana's a girl's name. You can call me Darryl. Or you can call me The Straw. But I prefer Darryl. 'Cause that's the name my mama gave me. And my mama was a saint.

Gilbert Whatever it is you're doing, Dana, it's not going to work.

Dana I'm not doing anything.

Gilbert We're still going to have to discharge you. You have to go home.

Dana Baseball is the only home I know and they booted my ass.

Gilbert I understand you're nervous –

Dana You know who I would like to talk to, who I have not talked to once and who is s'posed to be the best doctor there is, is this Dr Stanton lady I keep hearing about.

Gilbert I consult with her daily about your therapy –

Dana But I don't get to con*sult* with her.

Gilbert Because I'm your doctor and even though you won't listen to me when I give you professional advice, I do know what I'm talking about.

Dana All I'm saying is, I've never consulted with the lady. Also, I thought I got twenty-eight days for rehab. And also I have terrible cravings for booze and amphetamines and I don't think I'm ready to be on the outside. (*Beat.*)

Gilbert Fine. Dana. I'll ask Dr Stanton to come and talk with you –

Dana (*overlapping*) I had a slump and it's like nobody remembers the good times.

Gilbert So she can explain again why you can't stay because this is an issue of normalcy –

Dana (*overlapping*) I'm gonna make a comeback but I can't push it.

Gilbert (*getting loud*) Because as much as you might like it here, this is not the real world. And eventually, we all have to live in the real world. All of us. Even Darryl Strawberry.

Beat. She and Dana regard one another.

Dana I hear what you're saying.

Gilbert Good.

Dana And you're right. I gotta step up to the plate. And I mean that literally. Not as a metaphor.

Gilbert gives her a look.

Gilbert You don't have to explain it.

Dana 'Cause I'm a professional baseball player –

Gilbert I get it.

Dana I'm Darryl Strawberry.

Blackout.

End of Act One.

Act Two

SCENE ONE

Dr Gilbert's office, an hour later. Dr Gilbert is gone.
Dr Stanton is talking to Dana. Stanton is very maternal,
kind – a wise and gentle aunt.

Stanton You know you're not Darryl Strawberry.

Dana (*thinks*) Now, if you mean by that, who is the real
Darryl Strawberry? And is he me? Then yeah, you're
right. 'Cause the Darryl that gets projected out there, for
the world? That's not me. That's not real.

Stanton You're Dana Fielding.

Dana Nuh-uh.

Stanton You're Dana Fielding and you're very sad right
now and you feel alone and frightened. And you don't
want to go home because it feels very safe here. But we
have this outrageous, stupid, ridiculous situation with
your insurance company and the hospital wants to
discharge you. You understand that I don't want to
discharge you. But unfortunately the insurance companies
are making the decisions these days.

Dana Well, I gotta lot of money from playing baseball so
I can prob'ly just pay for it myself. I have, like, a million
dollars or something.

Stanton I don't think you have a million dollars.

Dana Six million dollars.

Stanton If you don't have a million dollars you don't
have six million dollars.

Dana I let my accountants handle the money.

Stanton looks at her.

Stanton Are you afraid you'll hurt yourself, if you leave?

Dana I might . . . do some drugs. And hurt myself. Like that.

Stanton What do you think the chances are? That you might hurt yourself? On a scale of one to five?

Dana (*thinks*) Four and a half?

Stanton Well, that's better than five. How's it been for you, talking with Dr Gilbert?

Dana Okay. She's a smart lady.

Stanton But?

Dana I think she's been trying to help me with some life strategies, or something.

Stanton She's working with you on what we call behaviour modification. Because she really wants you to be happy. She's very aware of your fears, but she also knows the reality of your situation, so she's doing just what she should be doing. In terms of these life strategies, as you call them.

Dana But most of 'em I already tried. (*Beat.*)

Stanton This is a radical question, I know, but have you ever considered another line of work?

Dana Every day.

Stanton And?

Dana See, the thing is this: I love what I do. Or I did love what I do. But it got ruined for me. And now I hate it.

Stanton How did it get ruined?

Dana Shit. Like every way possible, basically.

Stanton waits.

When I was a kid, you know . . . (*Trails off.*) Like if it
seemed like things were sad at home – like my daddy,
he wasn't good with money, and sometimes my mama
would get sad – when I was a little boy? So I would go to
the park. Get in a game. And I was really good at it. All
the kids wanted me on their team. And sometimes my
parents would come watch me play and I could see it
made 'em happy and I liked that. (*Small beat.*) But also,
I liked the way it made me feel. Like, I felt real confident.
Even if I had a couple of strikes on me, it didn't get me
down. I'd say to myself, 'Shit, just hit the next one.' And
I would. But even if I didn't, it didn't matter. It wasn't a
league or anything. It was just a bunch of kids from the
neighbourhood, running around, goofing off. (*Small beat.*)
But then everybody wants you to get organised and you're
in Little League and all of a sudden all the parents are out
there, screaming at the coaches and the coaches are
yelling at the kids and it's like, high stakes all of a sudden.
And then everybody's telling you, 'Turn pro, turn pro.'
And then, you know, your mama dies of cancer and your
daddy's long gone – 'cause he ran off into the projects
and became a dope addict or something. But the long
and short of it is, you hit a home run and win the World
Series and there's nobody there to see it. There's this
big fat party and everybody's all over you but when it's
over, you go home by yourself. (*Small beat.*) And then
everybody's, 'What's next? What's next?' And you're like,
'I fucking won the World Series,' and they're like, 'I don't
give a shit. What have you done for me lately?' So you
become totally focused on producing. Runs. You get up
to bat and it's not, 'I'll hit the next one.' It's, 'I better hit
the next one or there goes my average.' And then it's not
fun any more, it's work. It's ruined.

Stanton How long have you been playing baseball?

Dana Since I was eight?

Stanton Do you think you're making any progress here?
Toward loving it again?

Dana I don't know. I've been . . . sort of practising again.

Stanton Shagging fly balls, that sort of thing?

Dana Yeah. And maybe . . . drawing? It's been kind of
fun. The occupational therapy room here reminds me of
my old art room in high school.

Stanton Oh yeah?

Dana Not that I hung out there a lot. I was mostly in the
gym.

Stanton Right.

Gilbert enters with some sheets printed off the internet.

Gilbert All right, this should do it. (*to Dana*) What's
your lifetime batting average?

Dana You know, I don't think you can reduce a man to
a set of numbers.

Gilbert Then what position do you play?

Dana I play in the outfield. And I am good in the
outfield.

Gilbert Right field? Left?

Dana Centre. I play all over the outfield.

Gilbert turns to Stanton, as if to say 'See?'

Stanton It's hardly a textbook case. (*to Dana*) Darryl,
I'm going to contact your insurance company. This will
require that I change your diagnosis. But I'll make it clear
to them that you simply need to stay for a while longer.

Gilbert Boy.

Stanton (*ignoring her. To Dana*) Had you packed?

Dana Uh-uh.

Stanton Good, then. If you'd like to go on back to your room, we'll just carry on as before.

Dana (*pleasantly surprised*) Thanks. (*She starts to leave. Then to Gilbert, indicating the internet printout*) Can I have those?

Gilbert No.

Dana No sweat. Like I said, I try not to think about that shit. (*cheerful*) Catch you on the rebound.

Gilbert That's basketball.

Dana Man. Ease up.

End of scene.

SCENE TWO

The occupational therapy room. Dana is standing in front of a canvas with a palette and tubes of oil paint, mixing colours. Gary is still working on his drawing.

Michael Why'd you pick Darryl Strawberry?

Dana I don't know. I was reading that book you gave me.

Gary Do you even know anything about baseball?

Dana A little. But I don't know anything about his career. The book's just him and his wife talking about his family and God and rehab.

Michael Where is it?

Dana I threw it away. I didn't want to get caught with it. But I have to do something. Dr Gilbert was quizzing me, practically. 'What's your batting average?'

Michael Career was, like, two-sixty. Three hundred and something home runs.

Dana Is that good?

Gary Yes, Darryl Strawberry. That's good.

Dana Well, I don't know.

Gary And why are you painting?

Dana I just felt like it.

Gary But does Darryl Strawberry paint?

Dana He could. If he wanted.

Gary I can't believe you're pulling this off.

Dana Well, Dr Stanton was convinced. Or highly sympathetic. I'm not sure.

Gary Are they putting you on anti-psychotics?

Dana No.

Gary Because technically, they should be putting you on anti-psychotics.

Michael Maybe I should try it. I don't want to go home.

Gary See? Next thing you know, everybody's going to be walking around, acting like he's Eleanor Roosevelt.

Michael During the week it's okay, I just work a lot. But the weekends? It's like time stops. I can't go to a bar, I can't go out with my friends. Of course they probably don't even notice I'm not there.

Dana I'm sure they do.

Michael Whatever, I don't care. I just make a big pot of soup. It's really fun. (*It's not fun and he does care. To Gary*) I thought you wanted her to do it.

Gary There's a difference between doing it, and doing it right, okay? (*to Dana*) Like right now. You should be Darryl Strawberry right now. You have to be consistent. With everybody. A nurse could walk in here, hear you chatting, and boom! Cover blown. (*Small beat.*) Lifetime on-base percentage.

Dana What?

Gary Your on-base percentage. What was it?

Dana Six?

Gary In chronological order, list every team you played for.

Dana Yankees?

Gary Wrong!

Michael (*to Dana*) Mets.

Gary Who'd you sign with next?

Dana The Yankees?

Gary No! You're hopeless.

Michael No she's not. We can coach her. It'll be fun. She'll be our own Eliza Doolittle.

    Dana starts painting.

It was Mets, Dodgers, Giants, then Yankees.

Gary I think you forgot Betty Ford in there between the Dodgers and the Giants, and the Giants and the Yankees, and the Yankees and the Yankees.

Dana Was he always messed up?

Michael No. He was great. He was Rookie of the Year. Won all these batting titles. But then he got all fucked up. And he kept getting busted and going in and out of rehab. (*Shrugs.*) So the commissioner finally kicked him out of baseball completely. (*Small beat.*) But then he did get clean for real. And he went and played for this independent-league team.

Gary St Paul Saints.

Michael Yeah, it's like, the bottom of the bottom. It's not even a farm team. But he wanted to make a comeback. And he did, he was hitting over four hundred –

   Gary laughs.

– it was insane. All was forgiven, you know. The scouts came back and the Yankees signed him again, he was leading the team in home runs. Then in the middle of the playoffs, he got colon cancer and he couldn't play any more. Then he started doing drugs again and he got busted again – they finally sent him to prison.

Dana Why was he like that?

Michael I don't know. I remember, he went in front of the judge and told the judge he wanted to die. That the only reason he didn't kill himself, was he didn't want to leave his kids without somebody to take care of them.

Dana So I picked the most depressing baseball player on the planet.

Michael It depends on how you look at it. He never gave up.

Gary On the drugs.

Dana (*to Michael*) How do you know all that?

Michael (*shrugs*) I watch a lot of TV.

Gary (*looks at the canvas*) Your duck looks like a chicken.

Dana It is a chicken.

Michael Why a chicken?

Dana I grew up on a farm, upstate. We had a lot of chickens.

Gary And Darryl Strawberry grew up in south-central LA. The only chicken he ever saw was at KFC.

Dana Fine. I'll put a do-rag on its head.

Michael Put a hat on it.

Dana What?

Michael Put a baseball cap on it and then it will be a baseball-playing chicken.

Gary Put a bat in its beak.

Dana (*looks at the canvas*) Seriously?

Gary Darryl Strawberry would.

Dana No, he wouldn't.

Gary How would you know?

   Beat. She looks at the canvas.

Dana Fine.

Gary And put him in the outfield.

Michael With a bat?

Gary I'm talking multiple views.

Dana I don't want to do multiple views. (*Paints.*) Although, with baseball diamonds you get those nice greens.

Michael And the groundskeeper mows the grass so there are those stripes in it. Dark green then shimmery green.

Gary gives him a look.

It's nice.

Dana (*pleased*) Yeah. (*Starts to paint. After a moment, she begins to speak, practising.*) Yeah, I remember the first time I walked out onto the field at Shea Stadium. (*Gives Gary a 'See, I know some things' look.*) I signed with the Mets straight outta college –

Gary High school.

Dana Straight outta high school and I'd never been to the big city before.

Gary He played in the minors first. Texas League.

Dana And I'd never seen the great plains of Texas. I didn't have a dime to my name –

Gary He got two hundred thousand dollars as a signing bonus. It was a huge deal.

Dana I had two hundred thousand big ones in my pocket. (*Small beat.*) That was sure a lot of pressure. People asking, 'Who is this Darryl Strawberry? What makes him such hot shit? What's he got that I don't got?'

Gary Two hundred thousand dollars.

Dana (*shakes her head*) Sad to say, I didn't have the answers. All I knew was I loved to play baseball. (*She lapses into silence for a moment, paints.*)

Michael But that wasn't enough.

She looks up at him.

It wasn't. It wasn't enough.

Blackout.

SCENE THREE

The common room. Michael has put a tie on and Dana is trying to tie it.

Michael I'm sure I'm wearing a tie.

Dana You look nice. Sober.

Michael Did I mention how much I hate my parents?

Dana Yeah.

Michael They're only good for one thing: I can blame all my problems on them.

Dana They did fly up.

Michael Oh, they love family week. You can only talk when it's your turn, so they get to yell at me and I can't yell back. Last time my mom brought a prepared speech.

Dana I'm sorry. (*She finishes the tie.*) There you go. (*as Darryl*) You look phat, Dude.

Michael You know, I don't think anybody says 'phat' any more. And I don't know about the 'dude' thing either.

Dana What about – I called somebody 'bro' the other day, but then I thought that was racist. So I went back to 'dude'.

Michael Maybe 'man'? I don't know. Darryl Strawberry's a soft-spoken guy, I don't think he says stuff like that.

Dana But I've been saying 'dude' all along. If I change mid-stride, it's going to seem weird, isn't it?

Dr Gilbert enters around 'change'. Michael sees her immediately.

Michael Hi.

Gilbert Hello.

Dana Hey Doc.

Awkward pause.

I was telling Michael here, that you have to run fast to the base, and not change your stride, because if you break your stride, you can miss the bag.

Michael And get tagged out.

Dana Exacatackly.

Michael gives her a look.

Michael That's good advice. Thank you for that base-running tip.

Dana No problem.

Michael And I have to go see my family now. Wish me luck?

Dana Yeah. Good luck, Dude. Man. Dudeman.

Michael covers his smile as he exits.

(*to Gilbert*) So what can I do you for, Doc?

Gilbert (*actually shakes her head at the stupidity of that whole exchange, then:*) I was planning an outing for the unit.

Dana Can we go to the movies again?

Gilbert I was thinking since the weather's so nice, maybe we could do something outdoors. I noticed that Warren Park has batting cages. Did you know that?

Dana Batting cages.

Gilbert Yes. Wouldn't that be fun? You could go out there and hit some balls?

Dana Huh. Well, here's my problem with that. I'm afraid if I go to the batting cages, I might have a flashback. Like, post-traumatic shock syndrome?

Gilbert Post-traumatic stress disorder?

Dana Yeah. 'Cause baseball for me wasn't all candy and roses. When people found out I was drinking? They turned on me. They threw trash at me. They yelled at me. (*mockingly*) 'Darrrrr-yl. Darrrrrr-yl.' It hurt.

Gilbert I thought people yelled appreciatively. 'Darryl! Darryl!'

Dana Only if I did something amazingly phat.

Gilbert Like when you won the World Series?

Dana Like that.

Gilbert That must have been nice, everybody chanting your name.

Dana I guess.

Gilbert How many people are in a ball park?

Dana (*shrugs*) Fifty thousand?

Gilbert Wow. (*Beat.*) I've never had that happen, you know, fifty thousand people yelling, 'Gilbert! Gilbert!'

Dana Not even at like a, psychiatrists' convention or something?

Gilbert No. So? Batting cages?

Dana Well, here's the real thing. Contractually? I'm not allowed to do shit like that because I could seriously injure myself and then I'd be out for the season.

Gilbert Fine. I just thought it might be fun. Baseball is a game, right? I assume parts of it must be fun. (*Small beat.*) Because I never hear about the fun parts. I only

64

hear about how hard it is. Not about the trophies, or the chanting, or the stepping out of the dugout and tipping your hat –

Dana That hardly ever happens.

Gilbert But it does happen, right?

Dana On occasion.

Gilbert (*beat*) So I hear you've been painting.

Dana I've been painting chickens.

Gilbert Chickens?

Dana Baseball-playing chickens.

Gilbert Of course. (*Pulls a piece of paper out of her pocket.*) Well speaking of painting, I thought you might find this interesting. It's about an artist. Her name is Dana Fielding.

   Dana draws back.

It's a review of one of her shows.

Dana I don't care for that shit.

Gilbert But it's a glowing review. Six, seven paragraphs about how amazing her paintings are. How 'stunning' and 'vibrant' and 'inventive'. 'Complex.' 'Monumental.' It's the kind of review most people would kill for. There's only one sentence that's not completely complimentary. At the very end . . . 'There are some weak spots – some less than meticulous shading, a preponderance of reds . . . (*Small beat.*) But these are hardly worth mentioning when the work is as impressive as this.' (*Small beat.*)

Dana Bitch.

Gilbert Who?

Dana If it's hardly worth mentioning, why bring it up?

Gilbert Maybe to say that nobody's perfect. I mean, how many people do you know who bat a thousand?

Dana Nobody. It's too hard. (*Small beat.*) You're hitting a round ball –

Gilbert With a round bat. You've told me.

Dana The ball's going ninety miles –

Gilbert (*overlapping*) Miles an hour, I know. Only one in a million people can do it.

Dana That's right.

Gilbert And how many artists ever get a review like this?

Dana What are you getting at? (*Beat.*)

Gilbert If I have one wish for you, it's that you could learn to enjoy your success. (*Beat.*) What do you say we work on that?

Dana doesn't answer. Then quietly, like a chanting crowd.

'Darryl! Darryl! Darryl!'

Blackout.

SCENE FOUR

The common room. Dana is talking to Erica, who is having a very hard time.

Erica So then . . . does it come and go?

Dana What?

Erica The Darryl Strawberry thing.

Dana I don't get what you're asking.

Erica Dr Stanton says you need to be Darryl right now, but I thought you could be Dana with me.

Dana Is this, like, a role-playing game? 'Cause I'm not into that. (*Beat.*)

Erica I hope you don't think you sound black, because you don't.

Dana Man, you white people are all the same. Like all black people 'sound black'. What is that s'posed to mean?

Erica Is it because of the fifty per cent? Because that's industry standard and Rhonda only gives me ten. It's not like we're getting rich. Rhonda always says, you know, being a dealer is like being an ice salesman in an age of refrigerators.

Dana You sell ice?

Erica (*getting irritated*) No.

Dana Drugs?

Erica No, art!

Dana Huh. You know, I've been painting some pictures.

Erica (*worried*) You have?

Dana Yeah. Just for fun. They have this art room and I go in there and I paint and I like it.

Erica Good for you.

Dana It is good for me.

   Erica looks away.

You know, some people who've looked at these things, they think they're okay.

Erica I'm sure they're great.

Dana You don't sound sure.

Erica Well . . . isn't it kind of soon for you to be painting again?

Dana I never painted before in my life. (*Beat.*) You know, I could go get the things right now and show them to you, let you see for yourself if you think they're any good or not.

Erica That's all right.

Dana You haven't even seen them and you're acting like they stink.

Erica I didn't say that.

Dana Maybe you don't have any faith in me. Maybe you think I can't paint for shit. (*Small beat.*)

Erica Get them if you want.

Dana I will. They're right down the hall.

She exits. Erica looks around, then gets up like she's going to leave. Michael enters.

Michael Hi.

Erica (*doesn't remember him*) Hi.

Michael Erica, right?

Erica Yes.

Michael I'm Michael. We met when you were here before.

Erica Oh right, right.

Michael Are you here to see Dana?

Erica Well, I was here to see Dana, but I'm seeing Darryl.

Michael Oh, it's okay. You can still talk to her as Dana. You have to translate it out of the Baseball, but it's easy. (*quiet*) She has to stay in character when she's out in the open like this because people wander in and out.

Erica Well does she have to enjoy it so much?

Michael Is she giving you a hard time?

Erica I think so.

Michael She'll do that too. I think she lets Darryl say things that Dana wouldn't.

Erica That's scary, because Dana would say anything.

Dana enters with a couple of covered canvases.

Dana Michael, my man.

Michael (*to Erica*) Oh, have you seen these? They're great.

Dana She doesn't think so. She thinks they suck.

Erica I haven't even seen them.

Dana My point exactly. (*She uncovers the canvases.*) Ta-da!

Erica (*looks, beams*) Oh my God. (*Laughs.*)

Dana You don't have to laugh at them.

Erica No! It's a good laugh. Good laugh. (*Looks.*) They're *amazing*.

Michael Aren't they great?

Erica They're fantastic.

Michael I gave her the idea for the hat.

Erica (*studying them*) They're really . . . they could potentially be kitschy, you know? But they're not. They're different. I mean, stylistically I see you. The brushwork . . . but the tone and even the colours are so fresh.

Dana So you like them?

Erica I love them.

Michael I do too.

Erica I think they're a huge step forward.

Dana Thanks.

Erica How do you do it?

Dana Well. I had these paints and I put the paint on the brushes –

Erica No. How do you *do* it? How do you come up with it?

Beat. Dana doesn't want to answer but Erica keeps staring at her.

Dana Michael said, 'Put a hat on it.' I don't know.

Michael I think they're sad.

Erica (*not listening. Still looking*) Rhonda should see these. These could sell. (*Looks at them again. Getting excited*) I wonder . . . you know I wonder if she'd put them in the biennial. It's not too late. She hasn't put the catalogue together yet. I could still convince her. (*to Michael*) This is the gallery's chance to show off its artists, you know. The best of the best. (*to Dana*) It would be so great, even if you just had a couple of pieces. It'd be so great. For all of us. To say to people, you know . . . I'm not beaten. You didn't beat me. (*Looks at the paintings.*) I may be down, but I'm not beaten.

Beat. Dana looks at the paintings.

Dana I feel proud of them.

Erica So I can show them to her?

Dana (*hesitates, then*) I don't know crap about art, but if you think somebody would pay me for the things, I definitely could use the dough. I only have so many days left in rehab. Even though I have millions of dollars I still have to have the insurance pay and they're starting to make some phone calls.

Michael (*worried*) Really?

Dana Yeah.

Erica (*smiles*) This is good, Dana. Rhonda will be very pleased.

Dana Well, I hope this Rhonda chick knows quality when she sees it, 'cause –

Erica (*overlapping*) Wait a minute. You signed them Darryl Strawberry.

Dana Yeah.

Erica How am I going to explain that?

Dana Something needs explaining?

Erica If you don't sign it – I don't know how I can say they're yours. They're so different. Or if I leave it – people will think it's very weird. They'll think you've gone off the deep end.

Michael She is in a mental hospital.

Beat. Dana looks.

Dana Tell them the truth. Say you met this brother named Darryl Strawberry at the hospital. And he had these paintings of these chickens. And you thought they rocked. So you said, 'Put them in a show.'

Erica (*pause. Thinks*) Like an outsider artist.

Dana That's not a term I'm familiar with, but yes. Like that.

Erica You're some guy who thinks he's Darryl Strawberry. Because you're crazy.

Dana looks at her.

And brilliant.

Dana I'm just having fun.

Erica That's what so brilliant.

Dana doesn't like this, but Erica doesn't notice, she's looking at the paintings.

God, I'm so glad they're good.

Blackout.

SCENE FIVE

The occupational therapy room. Dana is painting; she's almost happy.
    Gary enters, gets his sketchpad and pencil and takes them to the table. He doesn't draw, though; he watches Dana for a moment, then speaks.

Gary What are you so happy about? (*He sits.*)

Dana Nothing. (*Beat. She works.*)

Gary Where's the drunk?

Dana Michael. He had a . . . setback. His family was here.

Gary Family week. That'll do it. (*Opens his sketchpad.*) He'll be hitting the bottle in no time.

Dana You don't know that.

Gary Seriously, what are you so happy about?

Dana (*stops. Smiles*) Erica called me. They've already sold my paintings. A collector came into the gallery and bought them on the spot.

Gary How 'bout that?

Dana Erica wants me to paint more. She thinks Rhonda's going to put me in the biennial.

Gary So the world loves you again.

Dana Well, I don't know about that.

Gary Sure it does. The world loves you again and everything's gravy. You're set.

Dana I do feel somewhat vindicated. I have to admit. She said the buzz was terrific.

Gary So this Darryl Strawberry thing really freed you up, huh?

Dana Yeah. It's like . . . you always feel like you have to get outside of your own head, to get ideas. But I never thought to actually get inside somebody else's. You know? But when I paint, I imagine I'm him and it's like, I see myself doing all these wild things. Like everything's new and I can do anything. I'm diving for balls. Throwing the ball all the way to home plate.

Gary You better not throw to home plate. You better throw to the cut-off man.

Dana Whatever.

Gary That's a bush-league throwing error, trying to get it home. You hit the cut-off man, he gets it home. Whap.

Dana Whatever. I'm just saying I feel like I felt when I first started. And I don't even want to talk about it any more because it's hard to get back to that place and I don't want to jinx it. (*She starts to work again. Beat.*)

Gary You afraid it'll quit working?

Dana No. I feel good. Dr Gilbert says enjoy your success. Let yourself feel good. And Erica said everybody was so positive. Just really excited. About the paintings.

Gary Right. (*Beat.*) This ever happen before? Where you thought you had it licked, but then it didn't last?

Dana No. (*Small beat. She can't stop herself, it's like she's talking to herself.*) I mean, it's a constant struggle. But the thing to focus on is the present and how I feel now. And not to worry that things will go bad. So you just have to tell yourself, 'Don't worry about it.' (*Small beat.*) Which is a little like saying, 'Don't think about an elephant,' but if I work on it I think I can do it. The thing to do is to not assume that I'll crash.

Gary Why do you assume you'll crash?

Dana Because. I crashed before. But that doesn't mean I'll crash again. Dr Gilbert says maybe I won't crash at all, maybe I'll actually get better. You know. Happier.

Gary You gotta change your world view.

Dana Exactly.

Gary And not make assumptions based on the past and what's always happened in the past.

Dana Right. (*Beat.*)

Gary Because this would be bad, you know, if this only worked for a while. Because what are you going to do? Every time you run out of ideas, try to kill yourself and go to a mental hospital and then pretend to be somebody you're not? That's not very practical.

Dana This wasn't some trick.

Gary Of course not. I'm not saying it was. I'm saying enjoy your success.

Dana Then say that. And shut up.

Gary Okay.

Beat. Dana paints, Gary draws. Stops.

Here's something though: when I hear people say, 'You should enjoy your success,' I always think what they're really saying is, the reason you don't know how to enjoy it, is you don't deserve it. Like, 'If I had your success, I'd know what to do with it. Too bad it's wasted on you.' You ever think that?

Dana No.

Gary Dr Gilbert might not've known she was saying that – you know, consciously – but I bet in her subconscious that's just what she was saying. 'Give it to me. I'm the one who deserves it. And I'd know what to do with it.'

Dana Dr Gilbert doesn't want to be an artist.

Gary No, she wanted to be a dancer. Trained to be a professional dancer but didn't make it, so she went back to school and got her PhD and here she is, sitting in her office talking to crazy people all day, but secretly in her head, doing pliés or some such shit in her little toe shoes.

Dana How do you know that?

Gary I haunt these halls.

Dana (*looks at him*) You're so weird.

Gary I've heard her talk about it. She tried out for a couple of dance companies in New York, and she didn't make it. Then she had a kid and you know, typical story. Shattered dreams and whatnot. So here you come in, the professional artist, and I'm sure she's thinking, 'What the fuck are you complaining about? I wish I had your problems.'

Dana She's an accomplished psychiatrist.

Gary No she's not. She's a wannabe. A wannabe dancer. Everybody's a wannabe something. But nobody has the guts to actually try and be whatever it is they want to be.

Because they don't want to find out they stink. Usually, is the problem. So they come up with a million reasons not to even try. 'It's all who you know.' 'Painting doesn't pay.' 'Playing the harp doesn't pay.' 'Nobody even reads poetry any more.' (*Small beat.*) Which is true, that last one. I've written some arresting poems on the subject of Kevin Bridges and nobody will publish the things. There's only one or two magazines that even accept submissions any more. And forget about getting a collection published, it's just your small university presses and they only put out one or two volumes a year, tops. All the major imprints are owned by multi-nationals now and all they care about is the bottom line. They spend twenty million dollars on your John Grisham, or what have you, and then nothing's left for the rest of us.

Dana That's not John Grisham's fault.

Gary Sure it is.

Dana He started somewhere too, you know.

Gary Yeah yeah.

Dana Why can't he be an inspiration? You know. 'If I work hard enough, I could be John Grisham.'

Gary No way. You think that? That's your problem, right there. Nobody's looking at John Grisham thinking, 'How inspiring.' They're thinking, 'Fuck you, Buddy!'

Dana Not everybody thinks that way.

Gary Who are you kidding? Of course they do. That's what I'm saying. The only way the wannabes get through the day is by convincing themselves that it's impossible to get anywhere, that there's no point in trying. But then somebody like John Grisham comes along and does it, and they have to face the truth: it *can* be done. It just can't be done by *them*. (*Small beat. Turns it on her.*) And that makes the wannabes sick. It makes them wish you were dead. And that makes *you* wish you were dead. And that's why you shouldn't enjoy your success, you should run away from it. Because the same people who gave you that death wish are the ones who are giving you that success, and you can't trust those losers. These are the same people who treated you like you had the plague whenever your career was in the toilet. The same people who flocked to your bedside whenever you tried to kill yourself.

Dana (*quiet*) Nobody flocked to my bedside –

Gary (*overlapping*) Of course they didn't! You know why? Because they were disappointed. They wanted you dead.

Dana But why?

Gary Because then the assholes can say, 'I am King! Not her. Not the one who makes things. But Me! The one who breaks things. (*Looks at his drawing.*) I know I'm better than her and I'll prove it. I'll drive her to fucking distraction.' (*Small beat. Picks up his pencil.*) That's the only way you can get a foot up. Is to make sure whoever's on top goes down. (*He goes back to his drawing, starts filling something in quickly, hard.*) And then stomp 'em. Stomp 'em till their blood flows black.

Dana looks at him, afraid. Gary looks at his drawing.

Hey, look at me. I'm drawing your favourite. (*Looks up again.*) Negative space.

End of scene.

SCENE SIX

*Occupational therapy room a few days later. Several
canvases are leaning against the table, facing upstage. Dr
Gilbert is looking at them. Dana enters.*

Gilbert You know you're really talented. You could be a
professional artist. (*Beat.*)

Dana Thanks.

Gilbert Dr Stanton wanted me to talk to you. Your
insurance company keeps asking questions. Why, if you're
MPD, don't we have you on commensurate medication?
For example. Are we prepared to face charges of insurance
fraud? Lose our licences. Small things like that. (*Small
beat.*) We need you to be Dana again.

Dana Who?

Gilbert Please, let's not start that again. (*Sighs.*) You were
right. You weren't ready to go home. But now you're
painting again, you're showing again. The woman from
your gallery comes around for meetings in the common
room . . .

Dana You mean that art lady?

Gilbert Erica Lind is her name. And she wouldn't be here
if you weren't Dana Fielding. The successful artist. (*Small
beat.*) So we'll continue to work together on an out-
patient basis . . .

Dana I don't want to go.

Gilbert We've arranged your discharge for Friday. That
gives you a day to make plans.

Dana You can't put me back out on the streets.

Gilbert Friday morning at nine.

78

Dana People will buy me drugs. They will. Just to say they partied with Darryl Strawberry. Just to say they got fucked up with Darryl Strawberry, man . . . had a forty and a blunt.

Beat. Gilbert regards her, waiting.

But I only painted these so I could stay here.

Gilbert No, you didn't. They're too good. (*Small beat.*) For once you're not arguing. (*fixing to go*) I'll have someone from admissions come by in the morning –

Dana I hear you used to be a dancer.

Gilbert (*surprised*) Yes?

Dana Why'd you quit? (*Small beat, then she answers.*)

Gilbert I wasn't very good.

Dana Oh.

Gilbert But now I get to help people. Or try to, anyway. I hope I've helped you.

Dana I guess you've helped me figure out ways not to kill myself. So. Congratulations. Success.

Gilbert (*quiet*) It is success. (*Beat.*) All right. I'll see you tomorrow, Dana.

Dana doesn't say anything. Gilbert exits. Dana looks at the paintings. Long pause. She's trying to decide what to do and then she picks one up and begins stacking them against the wall. Erica enters, tentatively.

Erica Hello?

Dana Yeah?

Erica (*sees the canvases and goes right to them*) Oh look, you've done so many. This is good, this is really good. Do you want to spread them out here? (*She starts putting them back out.*) The lighting's not too great but that's okay, Rhonda knows what she's looking at. So the plan is to wait until the biennial and then announce that 'Darryl Strawberry' is Dana Fielding. It's not that unusual, really. It's like someone writing under a pseudonym. It won't be a surprise, though, that it's you. People have been coming in to see the two we have and they just know – they're too advanced for an outsider artist. And then anyone who knows your work guesses and that's that. Word spreads fast on our little planet. (*Small beat.*) And everyone's very happy, by the way, to know you're doing so well. Especially Roy, he's just . . . well, I think he's relieved is what he is. (*Beat.*) So are you ready for Rhonda?

Dana Sure.

Erica Are you going to be you, or are you going to be him?

Dana I'm going to be me.

Erica Great. (*Looks at the canvases.*) Excellent.

> *She leaves. Dana stares at the canvases, no expression. Then Rhonda and Erica enter. Rhonda seems a little nervous.*

Rhonda I told Erica, this is a first for me. (*Hugs Dana.*) Crappy studios, people's bedrooms. I had one guy who painted in the toilet even. But for you I'd come anywhere. You look great. You've lost weight.

Dana Thanks.

Rhonda I'm so sorry you've had to go through all this.

Dana It was nothing I couldn't handle, I guess.

Rhonda Listen, I know you, and I know how you push yourself, but just this once I hope you can appreciate this and just let yourself enjoy it. (*awkward*) So tell me you're feeling better. You're feeling better, aren't you?

Dana (*thinks*) Yeah, you know. I gotta lot of people who love me. I've got my friends. I've got Charisse. And most important, I've got God.

Rhonda I don't know Charisse.

Dana She's my wife. (*Beat.*)

Erica She's being Darryl.

Rhonda I thought you said she was going to be Dana.

Erica It's okay. Just say what you would say, but say it to Darryl.

Rhonda There's nobody around, I don't . . .

Erica Trust me, it's easier. (*too loud*) Darryl, Rhonda loved your paintings.

Dana That's cool.

Rhonda (*also too loud*) Yes. They were very nice. (*Small beat. Back to talking to Dana*) I mean, they were inspired. What I said to you before? About capturing that – not a messy quality, that's the wrong word – but I guess a sense of play, maybe, or . . . Erica said it: a sense of freshness. Whatever you were doing before, that's what you did. That's what people are responding to. And you made some money, which is always good.

Dana That is good.

Rhonda So, I guess Erica told you, we're thinking of including you in the biennial. But before we announce anything I just wanted to see what else you've been working on. I don't want a repeat of last time. I don't want to put any pressure on you to show something you're not ready to show.

Dana Well, I painted about five more and I think I'll prob'ly have three more after that.

Rhonda Goodness. Are these the ones?

Dana Yeah.

Rhonda looks at the canvases.

Rhonda (*pleased*) Oh, well, these are terrific. Very consistent. (*quickly*) Not that they wouldn't be.

Erica And you think you'll have three more?

Dana Yeah. I did the batter and left fielder last time. Now I'm working through the position players. I've still got the pitcher and the catcher to do. Then I thought I might do something different after that.

Rhonda (*pleased*) Really?

Dana Yeah. Like, maybe the opposing team. Or even some scenes in the dugout, or the clubhouse. Like maybe the right fielder crouched at the dugout steps, waiting to run out and start the game. That's like a moment of hope to me. When everything's new. Waiting to run out there and start the game.

Rhonda I see. (*Small beat.*) And are you thinking about focusing only on the chickens? Or . . . ?

Dana No. Or not just the players. Maybe there are chickens in the stands? Or chicken umps. Or chicken hot-dog guys. If the chickens are playing baseball then I think the whole world must be made up of chickens.

Rhonda Right.

Erica It's very imaginative.

Rhonda Yes. (*Small beat.*) I wonder, though, if you want to think about other subjects. Not just chickens doing other things, but something besides chickens even.

Dana Like, goats?

Rhonda Or even . . . maybe not animals.

Dana No. I like the chickens.

Rhonda Then you paint the chickens. You paint whatever you want, of course. (*Beat.*)

Dana But?

Rhonda Nothing. It's just that with something as specific as the chickens . . . well there is a shelf-life for that sort of thing. Usually. I mean, with the blue dog, for example. At first everybody loved the blue dog but then the blue dog was everywhere, he was even shilling vodka on the back cover of the *New Yorker* and pretty soon people were selling T-shirts with blue cows or blue monkeys. It became a joke. It's . . . predictable after a while. And if you don't progress then soon people will dismiss you. They'll think you're all hype and no substance. I mean, that's the exact issue we ran into with your last show – were you a flash in the pan, was your work becoming rote? It was difficult for me because people were doubting my judgement. And I started doubting my own commitment and . . . well, it's so devastating to sign an artist and then lose interest. (*Beat.*)

Dana Are you saying you don't want to show my chickens?

Rhonda No, I'm not saying that at all.

Dana 'Cause seriously? The way I look at it? I've got something to sell, and either you want it or you don't –

Rhonda I want it.

Dana Then say that. But save your lesson in 'art for retards' for somebody else.

Rhonda (*looks at her*) Pardon me?

Dana (*indicating Erica*) Because she says the other two sold without even being in a show or anything, sold like that – (*She snaps her fingers.*) Which means it's a seller's market, which means I can find somebody else to take them who doesn't talk shit to me. Hell, I could probably skip the middleman and sell them myself.

Erica I would hardly call Rhonda Block a middleman.

Dana I'm sorry. I'm new to this. But if she's not a middleman, what is she?

Rhonda I'm a gallerist.

Dana A what?

Rhonda I'm the owner of a very prestigious gallery and by showing your work I give it a certain imprint –

Dana Have you ever painted anything?

Rhonda I did. When I was younger. I think I have an appreciation for the process.

Dana Okay. I'm starting to get this, and now (*to Erica*) *you . . .* what do you do . . . ?

Erica I help Rhonda find talent. I . . . I put the right people in the room together.

Dana (*to Rhonda, getting it*) And you own the room!

Erica Dana.

Dana You own the room where the right people come together. But wait a minute! Do you even own it? Or do you rent it?

Rhonda doesn't answer.

So you have your name on a lease –

Erica Dana! (*to Rhonda*) She doesn't mean it. It's not her.

84

Rhonda It is too her. It's so clearly her.

Dana You're Landlady Jones! (*in a high-pitched old lady's voice*) 'You can't come in my house unless you kiss my ass. Butt monkey.' (*to Erica*) That's you, right? Butt monkey?

Erica Stop it.

Dana (*pointing to her ass*) 'Kiss it right here.'

Rhonda (*overlapping*) Okay. I would have overlooked the rest of it because you are, I think, mentally ill –

Dana 'I know it's wrinkly – just pretend it's beef jerky.'

Erica Dana!

Rhonda (*turning to go*) Oh – fuck you! I don't have to listen to this!

She starts off. Erica grabs her. Dana says the rest over the following conversation between Rhonda and Erica.

Dana I'd love to see you do what I do. You'd step up to the plate, and everybody'd go for a beer. They'd get up and get a snow cone and smoke a cigarette and then they'd go take a dump so they wouldn't have to see your wrinkly ass make a fool of itself.

Rhonda (*under this, to Erica, reacting to being stopped*) What?

Erica I really think we should put them in.

Rhonda Well, of course you do. That'd set you right up, wouldn't it?

Erica And you too.

Rhonda God. (*Glances back at the paintings, irritated.*) Talk to me later. (*She leaves.*)

Dana (*yelling at the retreating Rhonda*) 'I'm the Landlady!' Bonk! Inside fastball right to the head. You're lying on the ground, twitching around like a squashed cockroach. Everybody's laughing. (*calling out, mockingly*) Lannnnd-lady! Lannnnnd-lady! You suck! Get off the field! You're stinking up the joint! (*waving an imaginary piece of paper*) 'But I have a lease!' Well, who cares? You're a fucking joke! (*Holds up her hand.*) But me? I get up there and . . . *hush*! You can hear a pin drop. Because everybody knows. I know and the world knows . . . here comes the man. Here comes the man with the sweetest swing in baseball. (*Yells.*) You hear that, Landlady? That's me! (*Turns on Erica.*) That's my history! That's what I made!

Beat. Erica looks at her, disgusted.

Erica Well, I hope you're happy.

Dana (*laughs sharply*) No you don't!

Blackout.

SCENE SEVEN

The Rhonda Block Gallery. This time 'Biennial' is painted on the wall and underneath it is a list of names: Dana Fielding, Brian Lamont, Salvio Ramirez, Layla Walters, etc., etc.
Dana is standing in the corner again, but she seems happy. Insanely happy. She's holding a small bottled water and looking around eagerly. She sees someone, off, and waves.

Dana Hey! Thanks for coming.

The person says something. Dana smiles, calls.

Thank you so much!

Roy enters in his black leather jacket and hat.

Roy (*tentative*) Dana?

Dana Hi!

Roy Hey. How are you?

Dana Great! How are you?

Roy Okay. I'm really glad to see you.

Dana You too. (*Beat.*)

Roy I hear from Erica that things are going really well.

Dana They seem to be going really well, yes. (*Small beat.*)

Roy Well, I'm glad. I really like your paintings.

Dana That's so nice.

Roy It seems like you're enjoying yourself.

Dana I am. Yes. (*She looks off, smiling.*)

Roy You don't want to talk to me.

Dana No, it's just – it's crazy with all the people and everything. But I'm really happy you came. That was so sweet.

Roy I wasn't being sweet, I just – I wanted to say hello, and for what it's worth, I'm sorry.

Dana looks at him.

I'm sorry – I shouldn't have left you alone.

Dana Gosh. (*She actually looks frightened for a moment, like she has no idea what to say. Then she takes a breath and smiles. Cheery again.*) Oh well, that's the way those things go, isn't it?

Roy I guess. (*He looks at her, puzzled.*) Are you okay?

Dana Are you kidding me? I'm a hit!

Roy Right. (*Beat.*) Well, so long, I guess.

Dana Okay. 'Bye.

   He walks off. Dana looks around blankly, smiles again. Rhonda enters, briskly.

Rhonda Here's how I feel about it: This is a business relationship. We don't have to be friends. I have plenty of friends. You're an important artist, it's good for me if I can show your paintings. I hope you feel it's good for you to be here.

Dana It's great!

Rhonda Then I hope you won't run off with Erica without considering the impact it will have on your career. You can set her up, yes, but the question is, what can she do for you? Whereas I'm a proven entity –

   Dana really does see somebody. Waves across the room.

Dana Michael! Over here! Come over here!

Rhonda (*sighs*) Will you call me, then, so we can continue this?

Dana I have an idea! You call me!

Rhonda Okay. Then. I will. I will call you. And now, I'll go mingle.

   She exits. Michael enters, holding his own bottle of water. They knock fists.

Dana Dude. You showed.

Michael It's packed.

Dana My pictures sold before the thing even opened.

Michael No way.

Dana And Erica found some old lady who'll pay me to paint more chickens.

Michael Like a commission?

Dana Exacatackly. A commission.

Michael That's great.

Dana Yeah. How was the meeting?

Michael You know. It kept me from drinking for three hours.

Dana One day at a time, man.

Michael I know, I know.

Dana You just gotta work the programme.

Michael I'm working it. (*Small beat.*) You enjoying that water?

Dana (*smiles, nods*) No.

   They laugh.

I gotta tell you, the great thing about this Dana character is everybody thinks she's nuts, so they don't want to talk to her. I can get rid of people in five seconds just by being nice.

Michael That's great.

Dana You just do the thing, like you do with sport writers. Real polite. Real upbeat. 'Darryl? Why is it everybody either loves or hates you? Why is that?' (*humble*) 'I don't know, Scoop. All I know is God loves me. And that's all I need.' (*Beat.*) I'm glad this art thing panned out. 'Cause I don't think the majors are gonna call after all.

Michael Probably not.

Dana Fuck it. God's got a plan for me. I just gotta wait and see what it is. (*Small beat.*) I think the Landlady might be right, though – maybe I should paint something besides chickens. I don't know what, though.

Michael You'll figure it out.

Dana (*looks around again*) You know, I'm done with this. You want to get some coffee?

Michael Sure.

Dana Let me go find my jacket. And take a whiz. I drank a lot of water.

Michael Are you going to use the ladies' room?

Dana Do you think I should?

Michael Yeah.

Dana Okay.

> *Dana exits. Erica enters, as if she's been waiting for Dana to leave.*

Erica Michael, right?

Michael Right.

Erica Right. I thought, maybe I could talk to you about Dana.

Michael What's up?

Erica Well, I wondered how you thought she was doing?

Michael Fine.

Erica Really?

Michael Fine enough. Why?

Erica She's not really talking to me. I mean she talks, but it's in this sort of super-enthusiastic cheerful, polite mode. Like a really polite robot. But I'm worried about her and I was wondering, does she talk to you?

Michael Yeah.

Erica And you think she's okay?

Michael Yeah. She's fine.

Erica Because she's really keeping me at a distance, with the robot thing.

Michael She's probably feeling a little self-conscious. Everybody knows she tried to kill herself.

Erica But she's so cheerful.

Michael Do you want her to be depressed?

Erica I want her to be happy.

Michael Well . . . I think she's happy.

Erica Good, then. That's all I wanted to know. (*Small beat.*) I just wondered though . . . you know it's always been our plan that when I started my own gallery, she'd come with me. But she hasn't said anything about it lately. I'm afraid she's going to stay with Rhonda.

Michael Look, I wouldn't worry about it. Dana needs you. (*Shrugs.*) And you get pragmatic after a while. You take your help where you can get it and your friends where you find them. How you find them. It's not like you can afford to be picky.

Dana enters with a jacket and purse, smiles at Erica.

Dana Hey! Congratulations are due to you! (*to Michael*) She got me a commission!

Michael I heard.

Dana (*to Erica*) We're going to go get some coffee right now, but first I want to thank you for all your support. Thank you!

Erica So I'll draw up a contract for that commission?

Dana Terrific! I look forward to it.

Erica If there's anything else, you know, just call me.

Dana Will do!

Michael Bye.

Erica exits. They watch her leave.

She thinks you're going to stay with Rhonda.

Dana Hell. I'm a free agent. They can fight over me.

He helps her on with her jacket.

Michael I had an idea, I don't know if it's helpful or not. I don't know anything about art or anything.

Dana What's that?

Michael Well, I was thinking, if you didn't want to paint the chickens any more, there were all those other animals you used to paint. From your comic strip? The tern. Contemplative Tern. And the gnat, whatever the gnat was. And the Ghost Bison. That one really struck me. I thought something about him was so . . . I don't know. So touching and sad. I really liked him. I thought maybe you could paint him. Or his decimated herd.

Dana stands there, staring at him blankly.

I don't know. It was just an idea.

Dana doesn't answer.

But you probably don't want anybody telling you what to do. I'm sorry.

Dana (*smiles*) No, it's just, I'm afraid I don't know what you're talking about.

Michael Your comic strip. That you used to draw. When you were a kid.

She stares at him again, deciding. Then she smiles and shakes her head.

Dana I wasn't into comics when I was a kid. I played a lot of sports.

Michael looks at her, sad.

Michael Right. (*Small beat.*) I don't know what I was thinking. (*Pause. Takes a breath. Smiles.*) So tonight was a home run. Art-show wise.

Dana Oh yeah. Good night. Stepped up to the plate, waited for my pitch . . .

She takes an imaginary swing, then clucks her tongue to mimic the sound of the bat hitting the ball.

Hit the long ball.

Michael watches as the imaginary ball soars into the stands, stepping in with the voice of the announcer.

Michael Oh yes, ladies and gentlemen, it's going . . . it's going . . . it's gone! And the crowd goes wild.

He makes the roaring sound of the crowd. Dana looks at him.

The crowd's going wild, let's see that home-run trot.

Dana smiles, then lightly jogs in place, head down, miming trotting around the bases.

'Darryl! Darryl! Darryl!'

Dana stops as if finished with the game, looks at him.

Come on, tip your cap.

Dana hesitates.

Tip your cap.

She grins. Then she looks up into the imaginary stands, the imaginary lights, and tips her imaginary cap.

Dana (*still smiling, still looking up, still tipping her cap*)
Fuckers.

Blackout.

End of play.